I
LOVE
HELVETICA
I Love Type Series
Volume Seven

CW01064943

Published
by Viction:ary

Edited & Designed
by TwoPoints.Net

Neue Haas-Grotesk
Brochure, 1959.
Designed by Fritz
Büler and Walter
Bosshardt in 1959.

I had never loved Helvetica. Despite its omnipresence, I really only noticed the typeface and used her for the first time as a bland system font on a Mac Classic for my very first piece of typesetting assignment as a design student. Although I can't blame my unrefined typography solely on the crude font, I avoided her ever since. Besides that, it was the early nineties when humanist sans-serifs were the type to use and Meta had taken over as "the Helvetica of the '90s" (Robin Kinross). A time when it was the order of the day to "hate" Helvetica. Some of my colleagues never got over this.

Since then, I practiced a policy of peaceful indifference and our paths never crossed again. Until 2007, when I was asked to research the history and development of Helvetica for a book and exhibition project on the occasion of the typeface design's 50th birthday. My work started out as a timid approximation at first, but the more I learned about the genesis of Helvetica's family, her background, the people and the techniques involved and above all saw the original drawings, proofs and corrections, there was a certain fondness growing inside of me. Meanwhile I find myself coming to Helvetica's defense every once in a while. Because she wasn't meant to be as bland and unrefined as most of us digital natives had conceived of her. In fact, Neue Haas-Grotesk, as the foundry pre-digital type version of Helvetica was called upon release in 1957, is a rather beautiful and soulful design.

Although being credited mostly to Max Miedinger alone, the development of the original Neue Haas-Grotesk in the mid 1950s owed just as much to Eduard Hoffmann, the then president of the Haas Type Foundry in Münchenstein, Switzerland, near Basel. By mid-1950s Hoffmann recognized a decrease in sales and appreciation for the sans-serif typefaces in their program: Französische Grotesk and Normal-Grotesk. Both designs, from 1890 and 1910 originally and respectively, looked rather dated in the eyes of the leading Swiss typographers who would rather the more rigorous Akzidenz-Grotesk released by Berthold instead. Hoffmann had,

hence, planned to issue a new sans-serif since 1950 but hesitated because of the conceivable expenses. Now with the conspicuous rise of the "Swiss typography" and the "International Style" the time has come.

Hoffmann commissioned Swiss graphic designer Max Miedinger, a former salesmen at Haas, to develop the new sans-serif which should be based on Haas' version of Normal-Grotesk from 1943. Through his dialogue with customers, Miedinger had a good insight into the market's demand and what could make a successful typeface. Work on Neue Haas-Grotesk began in early fall of 1956 with the Medium weight (the official translation of "Halbfett" by D. Stempel AG, Neue Haas-Grotesk's manufacturer, which other foundries may refer to as the "Bold" style), which was aimed to be presented at the Graphic 57 trade expo in June the following year. From very early on, even before the actual development began, Hoffmann consulted with prominent Swiss graphic designers and the weighty advertising departments of Basel's chemical companies Geigy and Ciba. It was clear to him that the success of a new grotesk would largely depend on the influential designers' response, because winning them over would mean that the large printing offices would most certainly purchase the new typeface.

A sedulous exchange of correspondence, drawings and proofs between Miedinger and Hoffmann took place over the subsequent months. Hoffmann elaborately documented the whole development process in a journal. The new design was continually compared to samples of Neue Haas-Grotesk's potential competitor Akzidenz-Grotesk as well as Haas' "old" grotesks. Its most unique new features were the consistently horizontal terminals, large x-height and the extremely narrow sidebearings. Never before were designers able to set type this tight. These features resulted in the typical dense, vigorous color of Neue Haas-Grotesk. The two men didn't always find common ground.

Many details were discussed over weeks and modifications did not continue until late autumn that year. Miedinger in particular was still not satisfied with the capital 'R' and considered forms with a more diagonal leg than the "Schelter R" that we now recognize as the "typical Helvetica". Also, the characteristic 'a' with its drop-shaped bowl got its final form only after the initial presentation at the trade show.

The response to the new typeface was positive throughout and Neue Haas-Grotesk became an immediate success. Miedinger promptly took up work on additional weights. However, the competitors weren't asleep. In 1957, French foundry Deberny & Peignot released Univers designed by Adrian Frutiger and German Bauer foundry published Folio, both for hand-composition. For machine composition, the Monotype system was prevalent in Switzerland with Monotype Grotesque.

Meanwhile the rivalry among the different Swiss design "schools" and influential protagonists of the Swiss Typography in Basel and Zürich was at its height but gradually grew into a rivalry between the new typefaces Neue Haas-Grotesk and Univers. Competing for the favor of influential designers, Haas countered Emil Ruder's bias towards Univers by commissioning leading Swiss designers like Josef Müller-Brockmann to devise its marketing materials, which was key to the success of Neue Haas-Grotesk from day one. Articles, ads and supplements were placed in all relevant magazines, and extensive specimens designed by Hans Neuburg and Josef Müller-Brockmann — most notably a costly binder called "Satzklebebuch" with dummy text in all styles and sizes — had made it very convenient for typographers to lay out the pages. But Hoffmann knew that, to make it truly competitive, it was important to make Neue Haas-Grotesk internationally available for machine composition.

In June 1959 Hoffmann took up negotiations with D. Stempel AG in Frankfurt, Germany, who held 51 percent of Haas' shares and manufactured the matrices for Linotype's composing machines besides producing (its own) foundry type (at that time). The Germans were skeptical. Only five years earlier, in 1954, had they adapted Haas' Normal-Grotesk for Linotype which did not sell overly well. Also the taste for sansserif typefaces was considerably different across the border at that time. With a list of 62 potentially interested Swiss printers, Hoffmann was able to win Stempel over. The name "Neue Haas-Grotesk" however was deemed not suitable for an international market. Heinz Eul, sales manager at Stempel, suggested "Helvetia", Latin for "Switzerland" but Hoffmann was not convinced, especially since a sewing machines manufacturer and an insurance company already carried the name. He counter-proposed "Helvetica", meaning "the Swiss".

In the beginning only the Linotype version, issued in 1960, was called Helvetica. The hand-set type had continued to be sold under its old name for several years, which made sense because the design had to be altered significantly to meet the requirements of the Linotype system. The Linotype machine cast one line of type at a time from a row of individual matrices which were assembled automatically by typing the text on a keyboard. One matrix holds two forms of the same character: usually either Regular and Italic, or Regular and Bold. As such, both forms have to be exactly the same width. This "duplexing" inevitably led to compromises, causing Italics to often appear to be too wide while bold styles, on the other hand, too narrow. Kerning was impossible, which resulted in the typical narrow 'f' in Linotype fonts.

In the case of Neue Haas-Grotesk the size of each glyphhad to be slightly reduced to accommodate uppercase accents. The italic was completely redrawn by Stempel, as Haas' version was regarded "not good enough". The Medium was made slightly bolder, and the spacing of all styles was adjusted, making the Regular "lighter in flow" and the Medium denser. It was not a premise that the two type-faces had to be fully compatible since they were usually not used together at the same size. Hoffmann had no qualms about the changes as long as the design and proportions were maintained.

The immediate success of Neue Haas-Grotesk and Hel-vetica put pressure on both Haas and Stempel to issue additional weights and styles as quickly as possible. Older typefaces were hastily tweaked and renamed to meet the demand for a larger family, leading to many inconsistencies in design and proportions between the various fonts (variants). The Bold Expanded style of Normal-Grotesk, for instance, was cast more tightly and adopted as "Helvetica Bold Expanded". Similarly, Commercial-Groteskhad adopted the structure of Superba, an Egyptian serif, but with its serifs removed and letters re-spaced before taken as Helvetica Medium Condensed, Bold Condensed and Compact (i.e. today's Helvetica Compressed after Matthew Carter and Hans Jürg Hunziker's revision in 1966). Only the Italic weights were entirely original drawings. This stands in great contrast to the competitor typeface Univers, which was planned as a systematic family right from the outset.

From the late 1960s further development of Helvetica was entirely taken over by Stempel in Frankfurt. They reworked Haas' ad-hoc additions — Condensed and Expanded — and added Light and Light Italic. Hoffmann was right. Creating Helvetica for the Linotype and the international distribution through German partners had contributed enormously to the typeface's success, especially in the United States where the Linotype was a prevalent composing machine. Albeit not very system-atic at first, the family grew into a large, versatile series of various width and sizes, as small as 5 pt, cast from extra hard alloy, up to the striking Poster styles — my personal favorite — in wood, aluminum or plastic. There were also several alternate characters available, most notably a capital 'R' with a diagonal leg. Upon customer request Stempel provided a third form of 'R' of a so-called "Futura-form", a single-story 'a' or a 'y' with a straight descender.

Helvetica. Ein guter Griff
Brochure, ca. 1959. D.Stempel AG
Schriftgießerei Frankfurt am Main.

Helvetica
Neue
Haas-Grotesk

Haas'sche
Schriftgießerei AG
Münchenstein
Schweiz

14

6

Helvetica /
Neue Haas-Grotesk
Brochure, 1963.
Designed by Hans
Neuburg and Nelly
Rudin, Zürich.
Photography by
Atelier Müller-Brock-
mann, Zürich.

Because of its widespread popularity, Helvetica was among the first typefaces to be adapted to a new technology. However, almost all changes came with sacrifices to the original design, for instance, the switch from metal to photo-typesetting in the late 1960s. For metal type, separate matrices were created to cast the different sizes of a font. This allowed the design to be adjusted for each size, optimizing spacing, proportions and weight as needed. Photo-typesetting, on the other hand, enabled the infinite scaling of just one master design. To preserve at least some of the adjustments traditionally made for different sizes, foundries provided up to four sets of masters to be used for different size ranges. Another problem was the undesirable rounding of sharp edges in the photographic process. To work against this the letterforms were drawn with exaggerated pointed corners and notches. Also, the width and spacing of all characters had to be reworked. While Linotype hot-metal machines had justified the lines by means of mechanically expanding wedges, the "space bands", phototype systems, as well as the Monotype machine, required the calculation of line-length and word spaces from the width of the characters. Because computing unlimited spacing variations was not possible back then, the width of all characters had to follow a rather coarse 18-unit system (later 54-unit). This again implied that all styles had to be redrawn.

When Helvetica was adapted as one of the first typefaces for digital typesetting — initially as bitmap fonts in the 1970s and later as outlines included in the first version of PostScript — many of the design limitations from analogue systems were carried over to the digital realm. The version of Helvetica that comes with every Macintosh computer today still retains the 18-unit width system from the phototype era. Many of the curves lack finesse and the Italic was created by automatically slanting the roman. The adjustments for different size ranges were given up for a one-size-fits-all master drawing and spacing. In 1982 Linotype set out to revise and systematize the hodgepodge of fonts Helvetica had conceived over the years. Adopting a numeric naming system from the former competitor Univers, styles and weights were coordinated and complemented. The height of capitals and lowercase were aligned throughout the family. Yet the wish for regularization and cohesiveness led to new compromises — Condensed and Expanded styles required squarer forms, which had to be adopted for the normal width, again sacrificing some of the personality of the rounder original.

In 2004 designer Christian Schwartz was commissioned by a British newspaper to digitize Neue Haas-Grotesk. He calls it a "restoration". With "as much fidelity to the original shapes and spacing as possible", he carefully redrew the typeface to match Miedinger's original forms. The family is divided into two sets — Display, which retains the characteristically tight spacing of the original's larger sizes, and Text that looks slightly sturdier and more loosely spaced for smaller sizes. Furthermore, he incorporated alternative glyphs for 'a' and the straight-legged 'R' which had been available in pre-digital formats, additional numerals and other amenities, but the essence of Neue Haas-Grotesk was preserved throughout. Alfred Hoffmann, son of Eduard Hoffmann and former CEO of the Haas foundry, witnessed and helped fashion the development of Neue Haas-Grotesk and Helvetica for over 50 years. When I showed him proofs of Schwarz's new Neue Haas-Grotesk he was delighted. "There can be no greater present for the founding fathers. Almost better than the original," he said.

Indra Kupferschmid
Professor at Academy of Fine Arts Saarbrücken,
HBKsaar & author of Buchstaben Kommen Selten Allein

Neue Helvetica
Brochure, 1983. Concept, Text, Layout by MetaDesign, Berlin/ London. Photography by Gotthart Eichhorn (Still-life), Otmar Hoefer (Airport).

Typeface in Use
Helvetica Neue Bold Condensed

"Helvetica adds to content the aspect of official message."

Scusate,
non ci siamo capiti
2009 — Artwork
Client Triennale
Design Museum,
Milano
Design Tankboys

Tankboys was invited to participate the third interpretation of Triennale Design Museum, curated by Alessandro Mendini. The brief Tankboys has been given, together with other participants, was to create a series of towers, with the restrictions that consisted in the same square plant and the same height. This system of towers, characterized by the multiple language concerning the signs, materials, cultures and objects, thought as a totemic symbol and spirit of the city, where the facades and the volumes will express, with their different languages, the aesthetical and ethical tensions of its inhabitants, their poetry and responsibility.

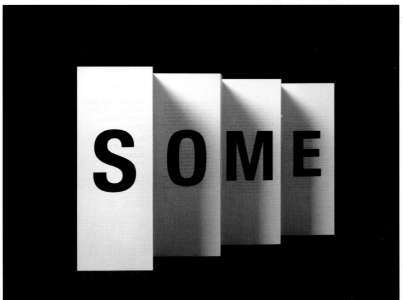

Somewhen
2008—Invitation,
Catalogue
Client Pulse
Design Tankboys

In September of 2008 Tankboys was asked to design the invitation for "Somewhen", a collective exhibition that combined the work of different photographers, under the common brief "Somewhen", a term that doesn't literally exist in the english language, formed by joining the words "somewhere" and "when" to mean a place in a time. As a matter of fact every work reflected upon the future, the time and the way the man is carrying on the planet. The unfolded invitation created the words "some" and "when" and showed "swohmeen", another word that played on neologism.

Typeface in Use
Helvetica Neue Bold Condensed

Je t'Aime
2008—Invitation, Catalog
Client Pulse
Design Tankboys

In May of 2007 Tankboys was asked to redesign the identity of a festival. Tankboys wanted to communicate the simple and well-known message: je t'aime. To add a little musical character and make it easier to remember, like a sort of summer-catchphrase (as the discographic industry every year does) Tankboys repeated the title four times (as the basic structure of pop music made of 4/4 rhythm): Je t'aime / Je t'aime / Je t'aime / Je t'aime.

Typeface in Use
Helvetica Neue Bold

je t'aime

Summer Student
Festival 07

Musica e dj set
Multimedia

Performance
Installazioni
No profit

4 - 8 giugno
Parco Fistomba
Padova

Entrata gratui
Free entry

Adbusters, Anthony Burrill,
Cai Shi Wei Eric, Allan
Chochinov, Delaware,
Daniel Eatock, Experimental
Jetset, Ken Garland,
Bob Gill, Milton Glaser,
KesselsKramer, Enzo Mari,
Bruce Mau, Mike Mills,
Bob Noorda, Peter
Nowogrodzki, Bre Pettis
and Kio Stark, Slavs and
Tatars, Stefan Sagmeister,
Filip Tydén and Gemma
Holt, Vignelli Associates.

Manifesto.

FOREWORDS — 16

hold back the final result for once and move
the attention on what is usually kept out from
exhibition spaces: the work process. Because
it's along the winding, potholed road that a
designer embarks upon every time he gets a
new job that lays the real meaning of every
project. By collecting and displaying these 21
manifestos, we want to suggest that only by
focusing on his or her own work process can
a designer fulfill his or her role in society: that
of building—or revealing—a meaning for what
surrounds us. Making sense, if you prefer.

Tankboys and Cosimo Bizzarri

MANIFESTO — 17

First Things First 2000,
Work Hard and Be Nice
to People, Idea Innocent
Originality Reasonable, 1.000
Words Manifesto, Worse
Is Better, Mini–Manifesto,
Disrepresentation Now!,
First Things First, Otherwise
Forget It, Ten Things I Have
Learned, Life Is Too Short
to Spend It with Assholes,
Barcelona Manifesto, An
Incomplete Manifesto for
Growth, Humans, Credo,
The Pesto Manifesto,
The Cult of Done Manifesto.
Slavs, Obsessions, Manifesto
Generator, The Vignelli
Canon.

MANIFESTO — 50

also see a lot of things we still agree with.
For example, we still believe that the political
qualities of graphic design are situated
foremost in its aesthetic dimension, and not
necessarily in the direct message it tries
to deliver. Furthermore, we are still very
interested in the idea of a graphic design that
refers to its own material context. And lastly,
after all these years, we would still never work
for an advertising agency. So in that sense, we
still feel connected to the manifesto.
Experimental Jetset, 15.10.2010

DISREPRESENTATION NOW!
[1] Disrepresentation Now! On the social,
political, and revolutionary role of graphic
design. More an attempt than a manifesto.

File under:
/ Experimental Jetset
/ Washington DC
/ Voice 2001 AIGA

[2] In his vicious 1923 manifesto "Anti-
Tendenzkunst", architect, artist and De Stijl
founder Theo van Doesburg stated that "as
obvious as it may sound, there is no structural
difference between a painting that depicts
Trotsky heading a red army, and a painting
that depicts Napoleon heading an imperial
army.
    It is irrelevant whether a piece of art

MANIFESTO — 51

promotes either proletarian or patriotic values".
    This quote can be easily misunderstood as
blatantly apolitical, but in our humble opinion,
it is far from that. In Van Doesburg's view, it
doesn't really matter what a painting depicts;
it is the act of depiction itself, the process
of representation, that he regards as highly
anti-revolutionary.
    Van Doesburg and many other modernists
saw representative art as inherently
bourgeois; suggestive, tendentious and false.
Regardless of the subject.
[3] Although formulated almost a century ago,
we, as Experimental Jetset, have to admit
we feel a certain affinity for Van Doesburg's
'anti-tendentious' ideas.
    Although at first sight it might seem
impossible to differentiate between
'presentative' and 'representative' graphic
design, we do think it is possible to make a
distinction of some sort.
    For example, it's hard to deny that most
graphic design produced within the context
of advertising is inherently representative; as
per definition, advertising never 'is' in itself, it
always 'is about' something else.
    Advertising is a phenomenon that
constantly dissolves its own physical
appearance, in order to describe and
represent appearances other than itself.
"Whereas presentative graphic design seems
to underline its own physical appearance,

Manifesto.
2009—Exhibition, Book
Design Tankboys

Manifesto., the project collecting the personal manifestos of some of today's smartest international designers, is growing and has recently complied into a book that design lovers can buy on-line. "Manifesto." was born in 2009 with an exhibition at XYZ gallery, Treviso, Italy. Its second edition was displayed in fall 2010 at Shandong University of Art and Design, China, with an expanding list of manifestos. Credos by Experimental Jetset, Milton Glaser, Anthony Burrill and many others have been included in a list that already featured names like Bruce Mau, Ken Garland, Mike Mills and Stefan Sagmeister.

The result of this work has now been collected in a 116-page book. Excluding the visual part of each manifesto in order to highlight the content instead of the form, the book was intended to serve as a small design Bible for anybody who want to know the answer to the question: "Why do you design?". Printed in 300 copies with a hard cover.

Typeface in Use
Helvetica Neue Medium

"For its neutral and rationalist aspect."

Typeface in Use
Helvetica Neue Bold

Which Venice
2007—Invitation,
Poster
Client Circuito Off
Design Tankboys

To promote a film festival Tankboys designed a series of posters questioning video makers the same thing: "Which Venice?". The question "Which Venice?" intermingles to create a unique typographic composition and the variety of possible answers. The poster, here printed in black and silver, was intended to grow into a coherent series, with one poster for each event using black and a different Pantone. The final results was supposed to be a mix of posters in different colors as the different answers to the question "Which Venice?".

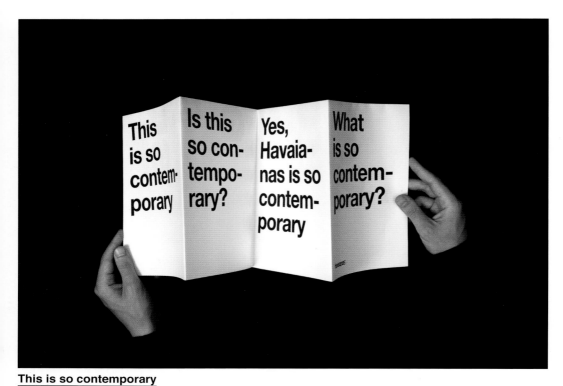

This is so contemporary
2009—Booklet
Client Havaianas
Design Tankboys
(Lorenzo Mason, Marco Campardo)

This booklet was part of an identity project for the fair booth of Brazilian flip-flop firm Havaianas. "This is so contemporary" is a quotation from a famous performance by artist Tino Sehgal.

Typeface in Use
Helvetica Neue 75 Bold

*"Because of its neutral
and everyday appeal."*

Love Mails
2009—Book
Design Tankboys
(Lorenzo Mason, Marco Campardo)

A collection of spam messages we gathered
during one year of work, with ambiguous
sexual sentences.

Typeface in Use
Helvetica Neue 75 Bold

Nina Klein agency
2011—Visual Identity
Client Nina Klein agency
Design Oliver Daxenbichler

Typeface in Use
Customized Helvetica Neue

The project was driven by the idea
to create a dynamic visual identity
dependent on size and shape. With
constantly changing dimensions,
the type design was set to reflect
a high emotional value of brand
recognition at the same time. The
design concept was therefore
reduced to a single customized
typeface as a new approach to a
strong corporate identity.

*"The straightness and
the huge possibilities
of customization."*

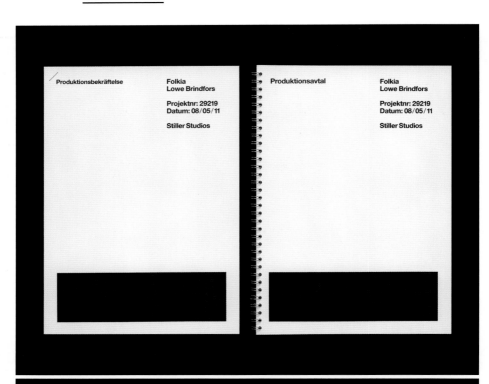

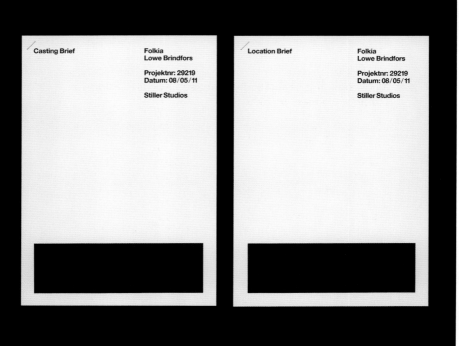

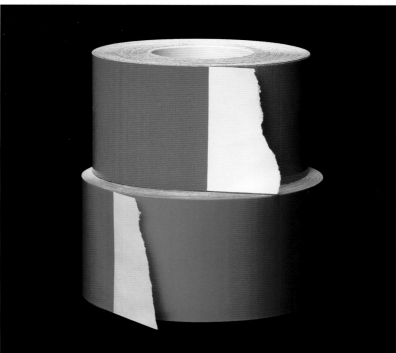

S

Henrik Nygren's
Favorite Helvetica
Letter is "S".

Stiller Studios
2008—Corporate identity
Client Stiller Studios
Design Henrik Nygren Design, Sweden
Collaborator Claesson Koivisto Rune Architects

Typeface in Use
Helvetica Neue

Identity for Stiller Studios (former TV-, radio and music
production company Forsberg & Co.) after their move to
a new building designed by Claesson Koivisto Rune, in
Lidingö, Sweden, in 2008.

*"Is there a better typeface
for an identity than
Helvetica Neue?"*

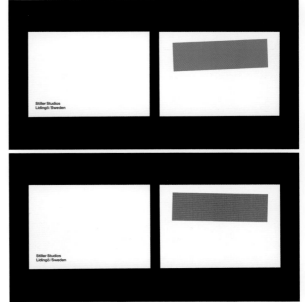

Åke E:son Lindman is a translator. His foremost task during the past two decades has been the portrayal of architecture. A subject that places special demands on the photographer and not only, or even primarily, of a technical nature. In many ways the difficulties correspond to those arising in a completely different field, namely translation from one language to another. Disregarding everyday linguistic contexts that seldom cause any great trouble – we have all translated a menu or a set of instructions – and thinking instead of more advanced texts, then the matter becomes rather more delicate. In many people's opinion, including the British poet and translator *W. H. Auden*, that which is expressed in poetry and literature is so intimately bound to its language that translation is simply not possible. Yet attempts are made – how could they not? – and in all their imperfections these interpretations create a rich tapestry of text and meaning. The concept of interpretation has a more open and provisional aspect to it than 'translation', which seems to promise an almost identical text only in another language. Inescapably, the interpretation bears marks of dislocation in style and meaning, however this is not necessarily a bad thing.

Exactly as in translation, architectural photography requires great sensitivity. It takes a delicate ability to feel and reinterpret a building's distinctive characteristics and furthermore to apply photography in making the almost insurmountable journey from a three-dimensional world to the picture's limited size and illusion of space. It is debatable what is left of the architecture and what is possible to convey through photography. What are we actually seeing when a picture depicts a building? First and foremost surfaces and structures – the building's exterior is featured and the outer façade becomes the face of the building. Details, rather than the whole building which seems harder to portray in an interesting manner. Light, space and volume are core aspects, as well as the flux between exterior and interior. Scale and size – two separate but related properties – pose a specific problem, due to the photograph always having a radically reduced scale from the original. Yet despite all these difficulties, architectural photography has become an indisputable genre and it is thanks to pictures in magazines and books that we see most of the more spectacular buildings. The question is whether architecture, in today's globalised and media-orientated world, could do without photography. And the answer is no.

Buildings represent a significant part of human history and the subject covers all sectors of society. Within its relevant photographic field, the focus is on architecture's aesthetic and expressive sides and the images are crucial to the professional process as buildings are designed, constructed, presented, discussed and analysed. Cultural history and art are important frames of ref-

Typeface in Use
Helvetica Neue

Pure Architecture
2010—Book
Client Arena Publishers
Design Henrik Nygren Design, Sweden
Photography Åke E:son Lindman
Text Niclas Östlind, Julia Tedroff

Book on architectural photographer Åke
E:son Lindman with three variants of covers.

"Is there a better typeface for a
book about architecture and pho-
tography than Helvetica Neue?"

P

Henrik Nygren's
Favorite Helvetica
Letter is "P".

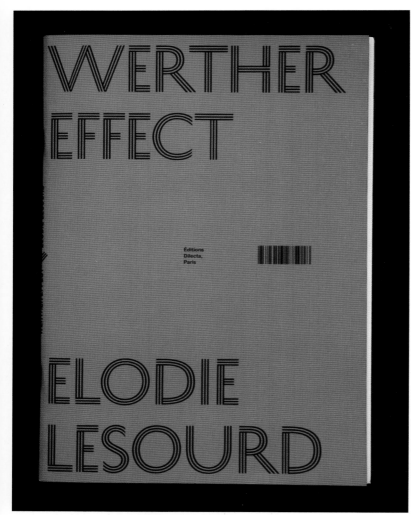

Werther Effect
2011—Book
Client Éditions Dilecta, Paris
Design Clément Le Tulle-Neyret

Monographic catalog for French
artist Élodie Lesourd, published
by Éditions Dilecta, co-edited with
Adera, Galerie Olivier Robert, les
Églises de Chelles and CNAP.

R

Clément Le Tulle-
Neyret's Favorite
Helvetica Letter is "R".

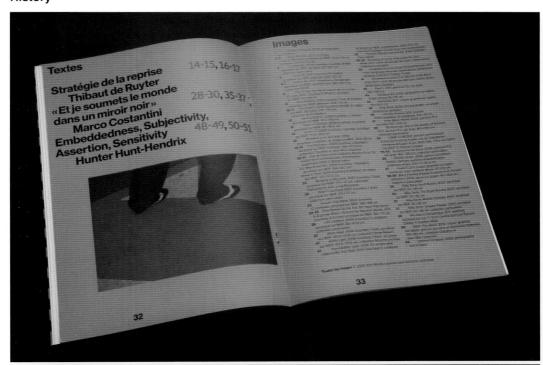

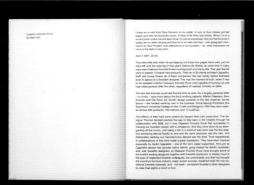

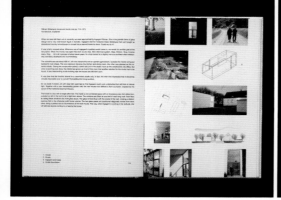

ARCHITECTURE
BIRKHÄUSER ARCHITECTURE CLAESSON KOIVISTO RUNE
INNOVATIVE BUT NOT DISRUPTIVE /PAULA ANTONELLI
PHOTOGRAPHY ÅKE E:SON LINDMAN
BIRKHÄUSER
1

DESIGN
BIRKHÄUSER DESIGN CLAESSON KOIVISTO RUNE
A TRIO IN A WORLD OF SOLO /MARK ISITT
PHOTOGRAPHY JOHAN FOWELIN
BIRKHÄUSER
2

Claesson Koivisto Rune Architecture and Claesson Koivisto Rune Design.
2007—Books
Client Birkhäuser Verlag
Design Henrik Nygren Design, Sweden
Photography Åke E:son Lindman (architecture), Johan Fowelin (design)
Text Paola Antonelli (architecture), Mark Isitt (design), Mårten Claesson, Eero Koivisto, Ola Rune

Twin monographs for Birkhäuser Verlag (Switzerland): Claesson Koivisto Rune Architecture and Claesson Koivisto Rune Design. Project included posters for book release in Milan, New York, Stockholm and Tokyo.

Typeface in Use
Helvetica Neue

BIRKHÄUSER
ARCHITECTURE/DESIGN
CLAESSON
KOIVISTO
BIRKHÄUSER
ARCHITECTURE/DESIGN
CLAESSON
KOIVISTO
RUNE
RUNE
RUNE

BIRKHÄUSER
BIRKHÄUSER
ARCHITECTURE/DESIGN
BIRKHÄUSER
ARCHITECTURE/DESIGN
CLAESSON
KOIVISTO
RUNE
KOIVISTO
RUNE

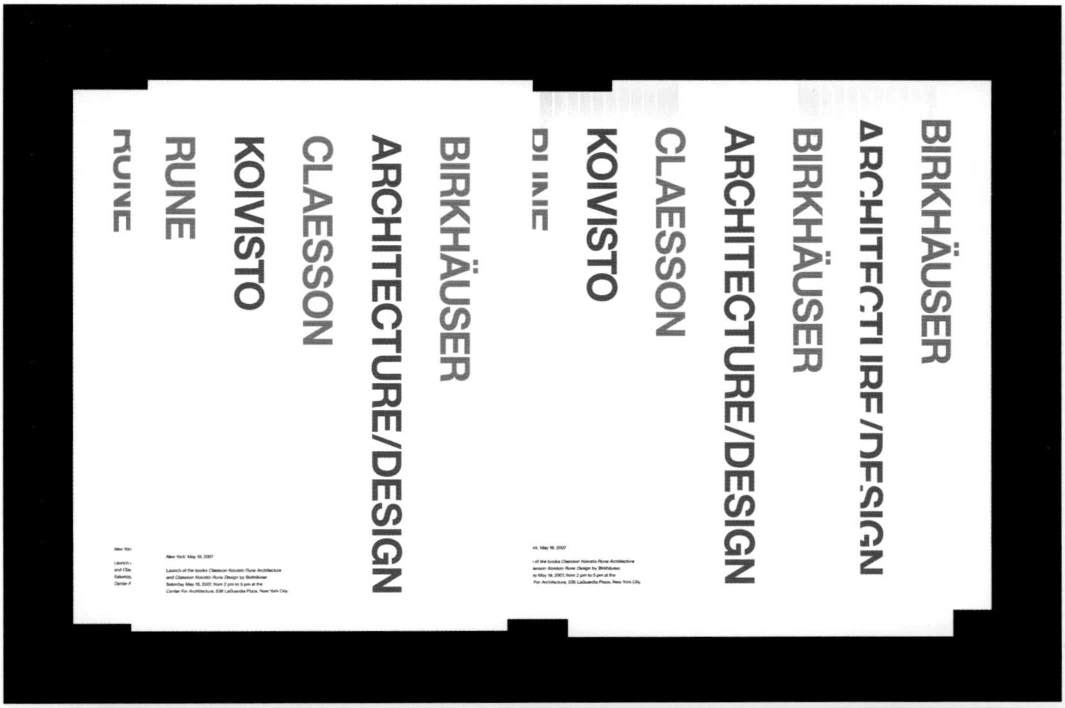

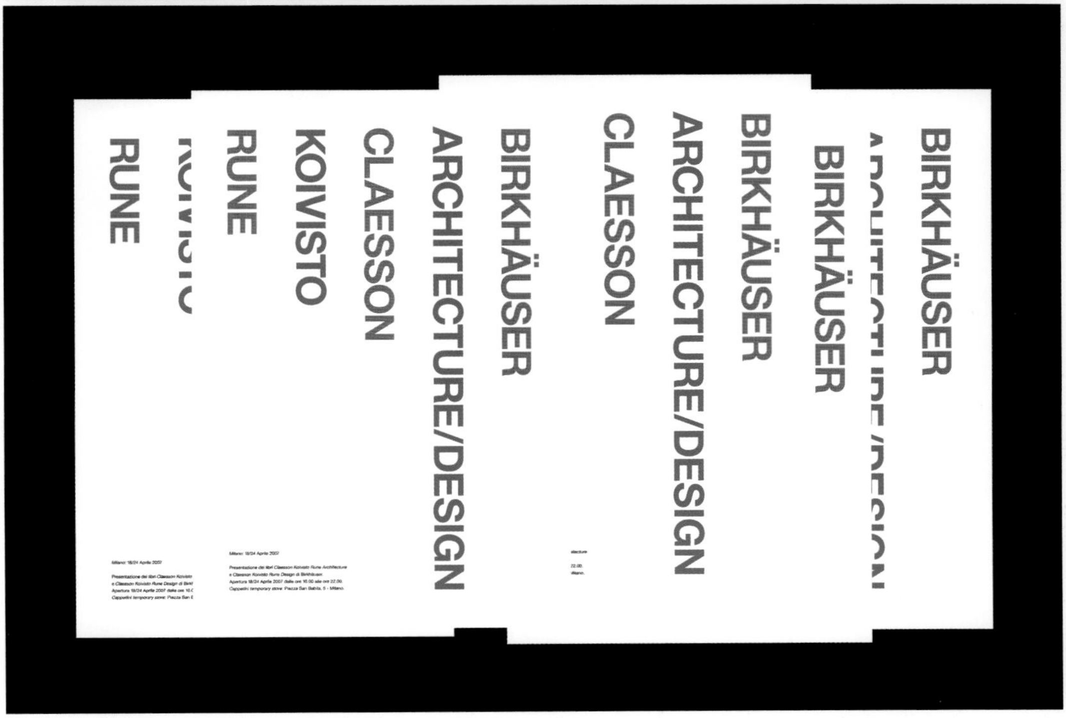

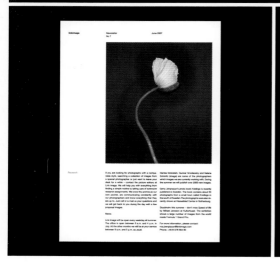

Typeface in Use
Helvetica Neue

Link Image
2006—Visual Identity
Client Link Image
Design Henrik Nygren Design, Sweden
Photography Andreas Ackerup,
Christian Coinbergh, Frederik Lieberath,
Gerry Johansson, Hans Gedda,
Lars Tunbjörk, Mikael Jansson,
Åke E:son Lindman

Identity and website for photography agency
Link Image, Stockholm.

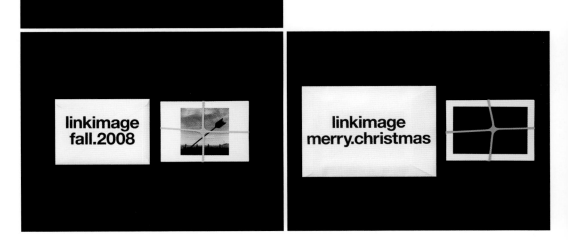

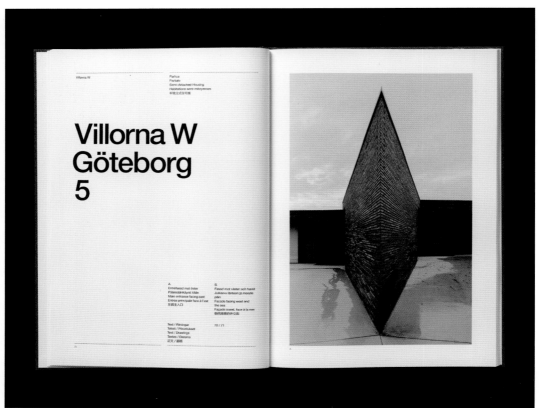

Typeface in Use
Helvetica Neue

Wingårdh Arkitektkontor,
Annual Report 2011
2012—Annual Report
Client Wingårdh Arkitektkontor
Design Henrik Nygren Design, Sweden
Photography Åke E:son Lindman, Ulf Celander,
Ola Fogelström, Tord-Rikard Söderström
Editing Gert Wingårdh
Text Gert Wingårdh, Jeana Jarsbo, Andres Lokko

Second part in a series of publications. Five
buildings completed in year 2011 were introduced
with text in five languages. The compendium
was produced and distributed to 700 recipients
around the world.

W

Henrik Nygren's
Favorite Helvetica
Letter is "W".

"Is there a better typeface for a
book about architecture than
Helvetica Neue?"

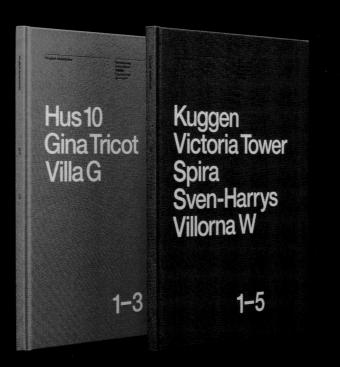

"I selected Helvetica Neue Medium because of its weight and contrast with the serif typeface I have used."

Typeface in Use
Helvetica Neue Medium

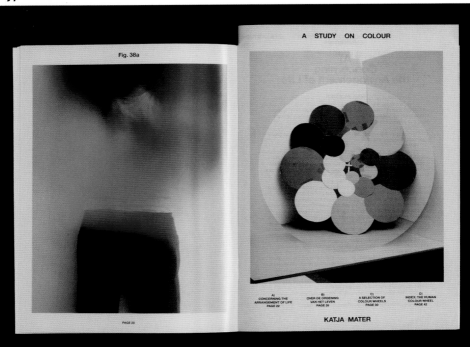

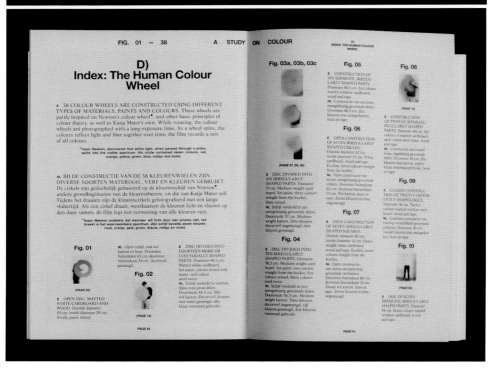

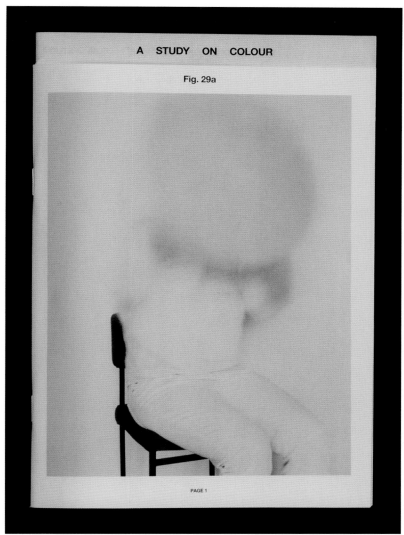

A STUDY ON COLOUR

Fig. 29a

PAGE 1

A Study on Colour
2009—Publication
Client Katja Mater
Design Veronica Ditting
Photography Qiu Yang, Veronica Ditting
Editing Katja Mater, Veronica Ditting

A Study on Colour is a publication made for the Dutch artist Katja Mater. The project was an experiment on photography itself, where Mater constructed color wheels partly based on Newton's color theory. While the wheel rotated, the colors reflected and blended light together, and Mater's photograph recorded a mix of all colors. The glossy, outer part showed a selection of those photographs. They were arranged as a gradient, going from white to color, then back to white. Mater and Veronica Ditting worked closely together and edited the publication. Will Holder wrote a text referring to the work, without explaining or self-justifying it. Another section showing the color wheels themselves.

RANDOM POETRY is a series
that deals with found words
and text fragments representing
in their entirety an ambivalent,
special kind of poetry.

The first issue of Random Poetry
contains a compilation of DJ
names, which were generated by
means of web tools.

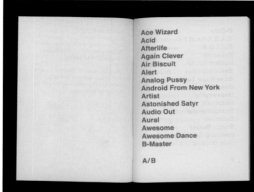

Ace Wizard
Acid
Afterlife
Again Clever
Air Biscuit
Alert
Analog Pussy
Android From New York
Artist
Astonished Satyr
Audio Out
Aural
Awesome
Awesome Dance
B-Master

A/B

Speedy Pants
Spinnin Elements
Splendid Lazy
Squid Fishlips
Squishy Wang
Squizz
Staggering Tizzle
Starmaster
Starrocker
Starwrecker
Stereo Bacchus
Stimulant Beaver
Stone-Cold Glamour
Stone-Cold Jupiter
Stoneface

S

Straight Slam
Strong Life
Stunning Neo
Stunning Sphere
Stupid Fat Bastard
Stylish North
Sunrider
Supa Kool
Super
Super Artist
Super Black
Super Love
Super Rough
Super Wolff
Surd

S

Random Poetry 1
Edition of 100 copies

Concept and design by
Sandra Doeller,
Leopold Lenzgeiger
& Michael Satter

Printed on a RISO RP 3700

Published by Random Press 2011
Frankfurt am Main, Germany/
Lisbon, Portugal
Sandra Doeller, Michael Satter
& Marco Balesteros

www.random-press.com

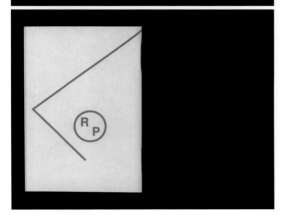

Random Press
2010—Visual Identity
Design Sandra Doeller,
Michael Satter, Marco Balesteros

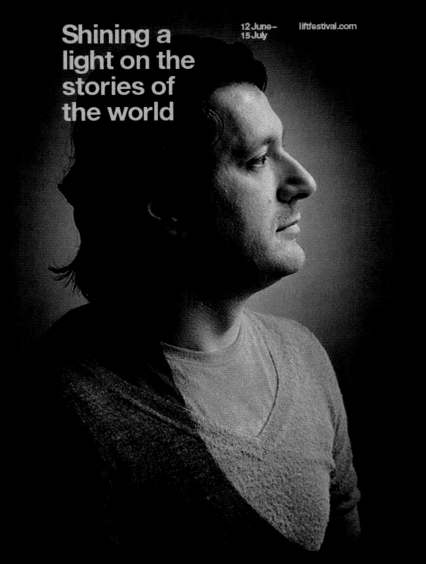

London
International
Festival
of Theatre

Shining a light on the stories of the world

12 June–
15 July

liftfestival.com

LIFT
Third Floor
Institute of Contemporary Arts
12 Carlton House Terrace
London
SW1Y 5AH

liftfestival.com
twitter.com/LIFTfestival
info@liftfestival.com
#Lift2012

+44 (0)20 7968 6800

Design & Art Direction by
Them®
www.them.co.uk

 Supported by
ARTS COUNCIL
ENGLAND

LIFT 2012
2012—Posters, Web
<u>Client</u> London International
Festival of Theatre
<u>Design</u> Them® Design (Dan
Moscrop, Matt Fisher)
<u>Photography</u> John Angerson

LIFT 2012 Campaign is an integrated web and print campaign featuring a series of portraits of typical Londoners in the spotlight. These posters were created and posted around London in the build up to the Festival launch.

<u>Typeface in Use</u>
Helvetica Neue

"As we had created a strong strap line for the campaign, we wanted to use a font that would be easily legible and create a strong frame around the image."

Them® Design's
Favorite Helvetica
Letter is "K".

London
International
Festival
of Theatre

Shining a light on the stories of the world

12 June–
15 July

liftfestival.com

LIFT
Third Floor
Institute of Contemporary Arts
12 Carlton House Terrace
London
SW1Y 5AH

liftfestival.com
twitter.com/LIFTfestival
info@liftfestival.com
#Lift2012

+44 (0)20 7968 6800

Design & Art Direction by
Them®
www.them.co.uk

Typeface in Use
Helvetica Neue Bold

Helvetica Poster
2008—Poster
Design Toby Ng

These brands distinct
themselves in their respective fields, but not their
logo font. Helvetica was so
popularly chosen to repre-

sent brands that it should
perhaps carry a trademark
(as it is awarded one in the
poster)! The red and white
of the poster served as a
hint of Helvetica's home
country.

(Answer: Switzerland)

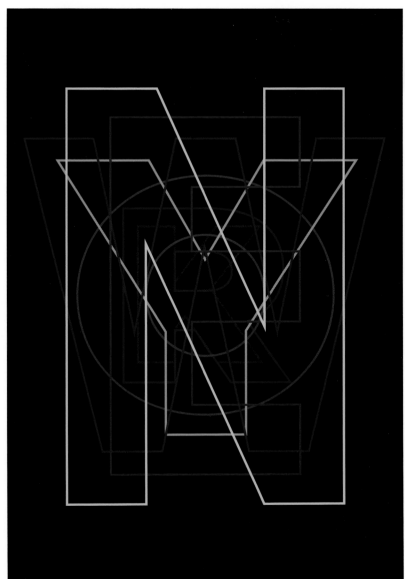

Typeface in Use
Helvetica

"Helvetica is used throughout the way-finding system for the MTA (New York's subway system)—a primary inspiration for these posters."

New York Poster Series
2012—Poster
Design Keith Kitz

New York City is one of the few cities in the world that is recognizable by its initials alone, and Keith Kitz strategically grouped the letterforms to allow the 'N' of 'New' and the 'Y' of 'York' to rest side by side as a visual clue to the viewer of these posters.

The outlined and overlapped letterforms represent the vibrance and congestion of the city and were inspired by the neon signs across the town. The linear letters are color-coordinated to various lines of the MTA (New York's subway system) as an added layer of visual connection.

Typeface in Use
Helvetica

Eastern Electrics
2008-10—Posters, Flyer
Client Eastern Electrics
Design Bunch

Various campaigns for cutting edge
music event Eastern Electrics.

Bunch's Favorite
Helvetica Letter is "I".

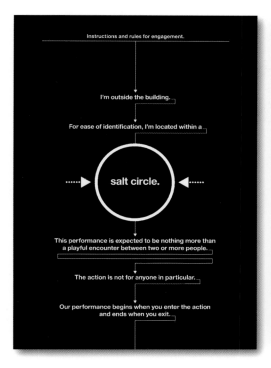

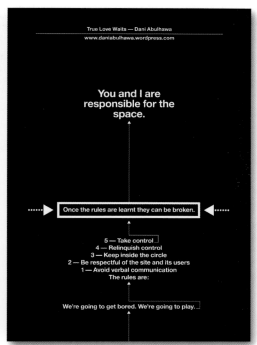

"Information-led design with instruc-tions needs to be clear, concise and informative."

Loose Collective's
Favorite Helvetica
Letter is "a".

True Love Waits
2012—Flyer
Client Dani Abulhawa
Design Loose Collective (Graham Jones)

Dani Abulhawa is a performance artist who explores gendered play in public urban spaces. Instructional, information-led flyers were created to accompany a performance called "True Love Waits" by Abulhawa as part of the exhibition "Tempting Failure" held in London. The piece involved the participation of the audience so these flyers were pro-duced to instruct them. The design is minimal and information heavy to convey clarity, but with a playfulness that conveys the tone of Abulhawa's work.

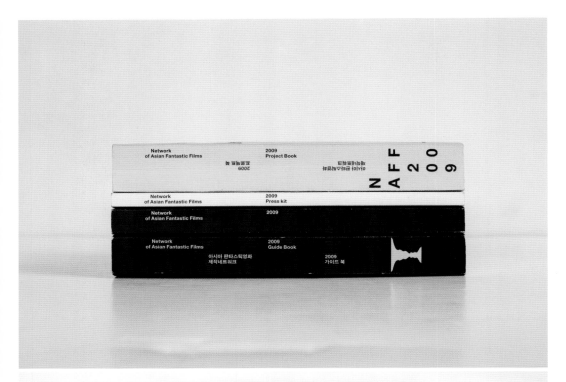

Network
of Asian
Fantastic
Films

19–23 July
2009
Bucheon,
Korea

20–23 July
It Project

17–23 July
Fantastic Film
School

naff2009.pifan.com

Presented by
13th Puchon Int'l
Fantastic
Film Festival

R

Workroom's Favorite
Helvetica Letter is "R".

NAFF2009
2009—Poster, Book
Client Network of
Asian Fantastic Films
Design Workroom

"NAFF (Network of Asian Fantastic Film) is the only case that we used Helvetica for our project. This is true. Actually, we don't like Helvetica. However, it's not that we can clearly say "I hate Helvetica" like Matin Majoor. Perhaps, we just feel grumpy because too many people like the typeface. The choice of Helvetica for this project was quite impulsive. Univers 65 was somewhat heavy, and Akzidenz Grotesk Bold seemed to be a bit boastful. That doesn't mean we had to use Helvetica, though. Was it in good harmony with yellow? That sounds plausible at least."

Network
of Asian
Fantastic
Films

19–23 July
2009
Bucheon,
Korea

20–23 July
It Project

17–23 July
Fantastic Film
School

www.pifan.com/
naff

Presented by
13th Puchon Int'l
Fantastic
Film Festival

PiFan2009

a
project

fantastic
film
school

N
A F F
2
0 0
9

Typeface in Use
Helvetica Neue 55 Roman,
Helvetica Neue 65 Medium,
Helvetica Neue 75 Bold,
Helvetica Neue 85 Heavy

Christien Meindertsma

Zeeuws Museum

12.11 '11-23.09 '12

Kavel Gz 59-west

Abdij (plein), Middelburg
www.zeeuwsmuseum.nl

Typeface in Use
Customized Helvetica,
Nobel Open

"Helvetica was chosen as a reference to the labels that are used by farmers that Christien Meindertsma was working with; they were all default set in Helvetica. The Nobel Open was used as a reference to textile structures.

Camden Tenant
2004-06—Newsletters
Client Camden Federation of Tenants and
Residents Associations
Design Carsten Klein

Camden Tenant is a publication written by,
and for, residents of Camden Town in London. Published four times a year since 1972,
Camden Tenant was looking for a complete
re-design in 2004. Where Camden Tenant is a
non-profit organization with restricted finan-
cial means, Carsten Klein looked to elevate
the publication from a throwaway photocopy-
style newspaper to an A4 leaflet that one
may want to keep and collect instead. Very
different styles in sources (photography and
copy) asked for unification by means of strict
typography and a dual-color scheme.

*"The Camden Tenant was ask-
ing for a serious, no-nonsense
approach – an idea which Helvetica visually supports."*

Typeface in Use
Helvetica Neue 75 Bold,
Helvetica Neue 55 Roman,
Helvetica Neue 85 Heavy

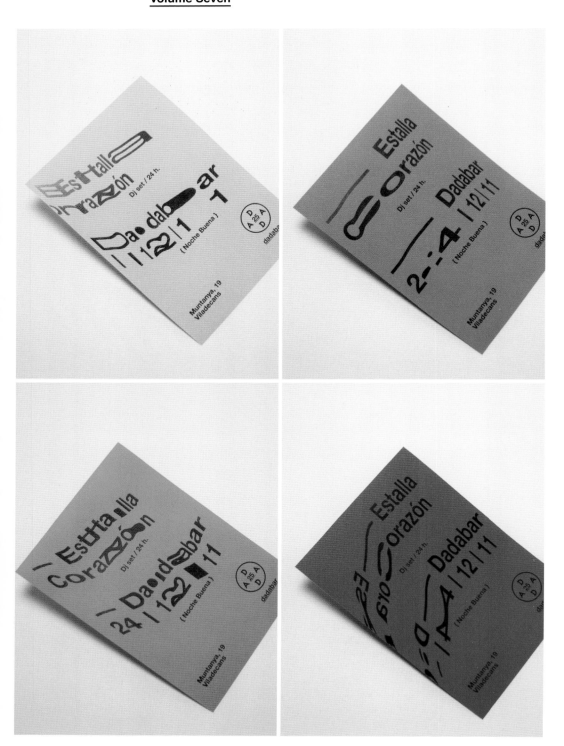

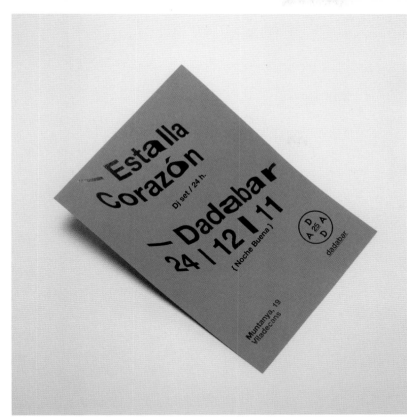

Typeface in Use
Helvetica Bold

a

Andrés Requena's
Favorite Helvetica
Letter is "a".

Estalla Corazón
2011—Flyers, Posters
Client Dadabar
Design Andrés Requena

Flyers and posters for dj set de Estalla
Corazón, on 24 December at the Dadabar.
The night will be so promisingly good that
even the types dance.

"I wanted a rational and skeptical
typeface which holds up after
being taken over by the scanner."

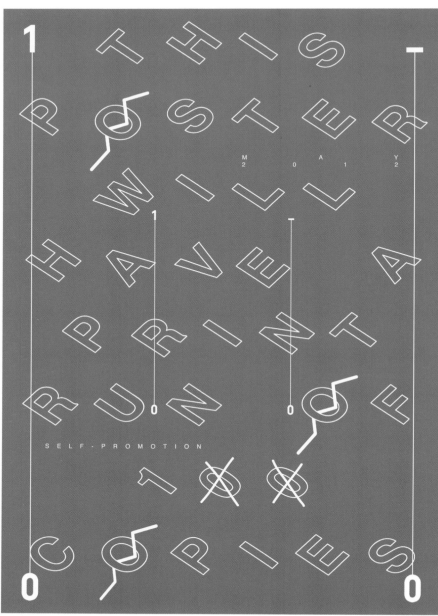

"In the elaboration of the project, Helvetica was surely the most linear, the most direct and the simplest font to understand in the complexity of the development of the lettering."

1/100 copies
2012—Poster
Design Walter Santomauro

The poster is a self-initiated work realized to promote a young graphic designer's project. The idea behind the poster derives from the situation what a graphic designer usually has whenever

he gives life to a project: the print run. The poster says "this poster will have a print run of 100 copies" and it is the spokesman of the future designer's works. In fact the poster could be printed in 100 or 1 copy as well. The number of possible interested clients will make the difference.

Red Bull Music Academy presents
12×12 at The Scala

Red Bull Music
Academy London 2010
2010—Branding,
Poster, Flyer
Client Red Bull Music
Academy London
Design Bunch
Illustration James
Joyce

Red Bull Music Academy commissioned Bunch to design the branding for their London 2010 event. The existing brand image was developed significantly for a new range of applications and purposes — buses, flyers, posters, banners and many more. Each event also had its own artwork produced by selected artists and designers from around the world.

92   CHAPTER FOUR   BOOKSHELVES   93

Talking about shelves, design culture and astronauts

Marc Berthier

Industrial designer and utopian

TEXT
RUJANA REBERNJAK

PHOTOGRAPHY
SEAN MICHAEL BEOLCHINI

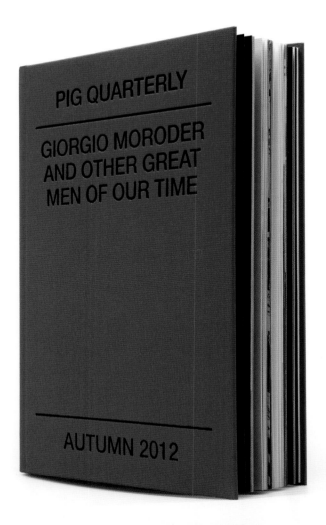

PIG QUARTERLY

GIORGIO MORODER
AND OTHER GREAT
MEN OF OUR TIME

AUTUMN 2012

W

Pig Quarterly
2012—Magazine
Client Pig Magazine
Design Tankboys (Lorenzo
Mason, Marco Campardo)

Typeface in Use
Times Medium,
Helvetica Medium

Tankboys' Favorite
Helvetica Letter is "W".

Tankboys redesigned the famous
Italian magazine Pig and they
wanted to use the most basic and
common typeface. Times and
Helvetica were chosen, both in
medium weight.

*"Because of its neutral
and everyday appeal."*

Paustian Furniture
Branding
Client Paustian
Furniture
Design Homework

Paustian Furniture House is a place of inspiration. They offer one of Denmark's largest selection of high quality furniture, carpets, lighting and accessories, the best of interior design from Scandinavia and from the rest of the world. The cornerstone of Paustian are design, innovation and high quality. These ideas are manifested in their house from 1987 on the Copenhagen waterfront, designed by the renowned architect Jørn Utzon. The unique Paustian furniture collection is also sold through a few carefully selected dealers in a number of countries all over the world, as well as several Danish and multinational companies. Paustian total design solutions is worldwide.

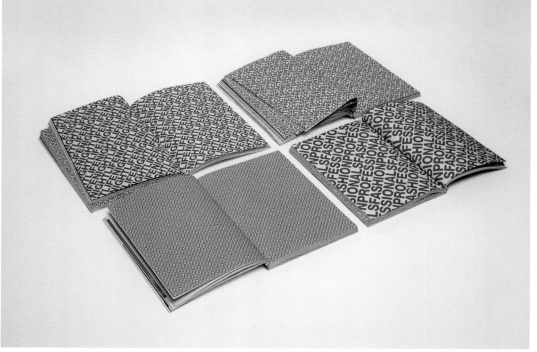

Copenhagen Fashion Week
Visual Identity
Client Copenhagen Fashion Week
Design Homework

Copenhagen is host to Northern Europe's largest fashion event, Copenhagen Fashion Week. On the catwalks are a growing number of new and known Danish talents with a preview of their upcoming collections, attracting over 2300 international brand name collections, more than 50,000 buyers, designers and global press to attend Copenhagen Fashion Week twice a year. Copenhagen Fashion Week is organized by the Danish Fashion Institute — a newly founded network organization created by and for the Danish fashion industry. The purpose is to develop an extensive network of industry professionals to promote, market and drive Danish fashion forward. In close cooperation with trade fairs, interest organizations, national organizations, event agencies and media partners, Copenhagen Fashion Week is a pivotal player in positioning Copenhagen as a fashion destination on the international arena.

GAS Interface Co. Ltd.
Client GAS Interface Co. Ltd.
Design Homework

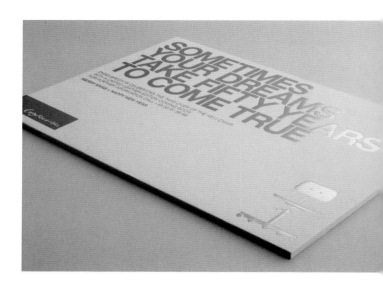

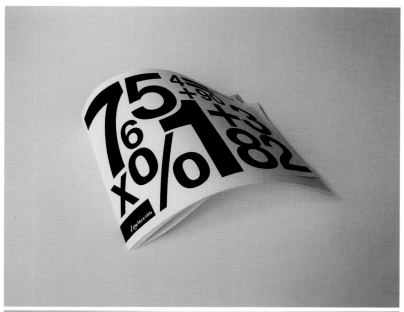

Engelbrechts Furniture
Invitation, Catalog
Client Engelbrechts Furniture
Design Homework

Engelbrechts is a furniture manu-
facturer, who works in collabora-
tion with designers such as Erik
Magnussen, Jørgen Rasmussen,
Vilhelm Lauritzen Architects, and
Kasper Salto.

Holland Festival
2009—Poster
Client
Holland Festival
Design
Maureen Mooren

Poster campaign for
the annual Holland
Festival.

Typeface in Use
Helvetica Neue TT Bold,
DTL Elzevir T Caps Regular,
ITC Avant Garde Gothic BT Extra Light,
Shatter Let Plain

Holland Festival
2010—Poster
Client Holland Festival
Design Maureen Mooren

Typeface in Use
Helvetica Neue TT Bold,
DTL Elzevir T Caps Regular,
Poplar Std Black

69

I − 23 JUNI 2010

FLUX

HOLLAND

FESTIVAL

HOLLAND

FESTIVAL

1 — 23 JUNI 2010

FLUX

HOLLAND

HOLLAND

FESTIVAL

HOLLAND

FESTIVAL

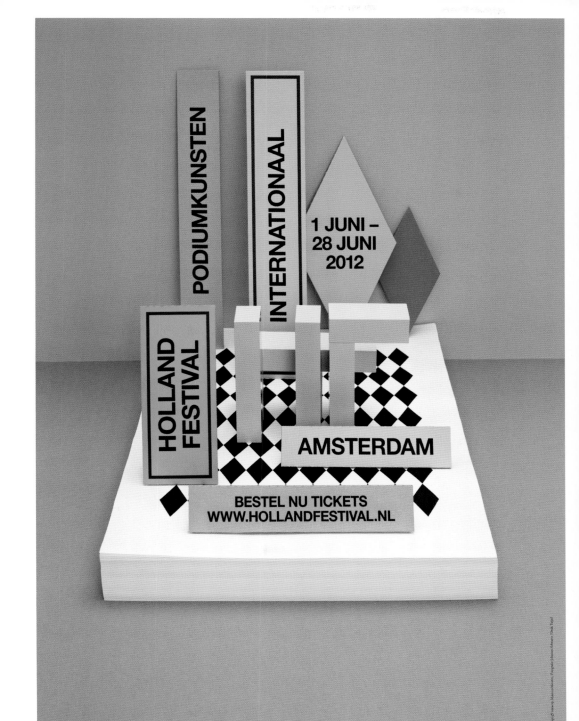

Holland Festival
2012—Poster
Client Holland Festival

Design Maureen Mooren
Photography Johannes
Schwartz

Typeface in Use
Helvetica Neue TT Bold

Kapulica Studio
2007—Visual Identity
Client **Kapulica Studio**
Design **Bunch**

**Kapulica is a creative
event agency. To pres-
ent the creative nature
of the studio, Bunch
used the 'K' as the
message medium. A
dozens of 'K' were
applied across the
identity with relevance
to respective applica-
tions. The letterhead
was kept simple
and official with a
varnished 'K', while
the business cards
carried a black 'K'
which can pop open
to reveal an illustrated
'K' beneath.**

Munich Techno
2011—Event Identity
Client Munich Techno
Design C100 Purple Haze

C100 Purple Haze was responsible for the entire visual appearance of Munich Techno, a monthly club night. The package includes conception, guidance, corporate identity and poster design.

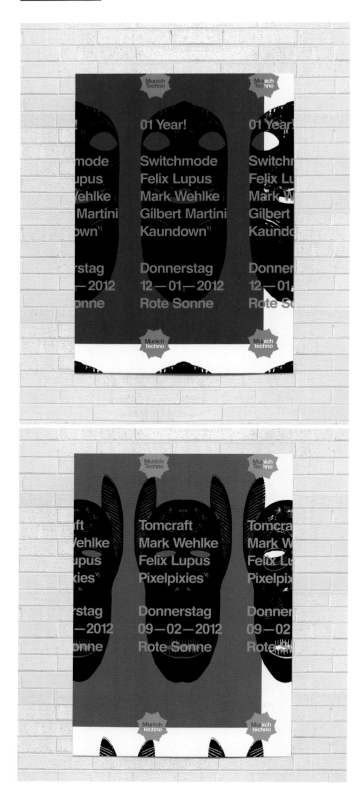

Typeface in Use
Helvetica Bold

"Helvetica and techno music, a timeless symbiosis."

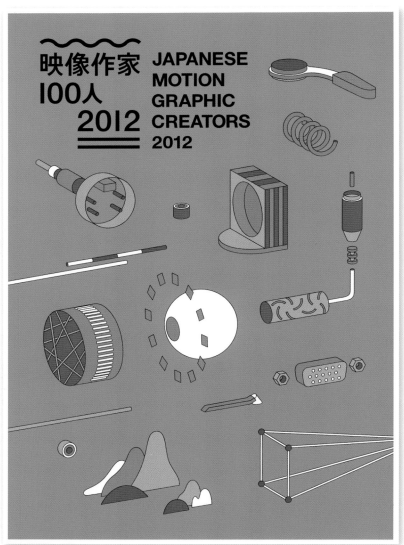

"We wanted to used simple fonts that lead people's attention more to the visuals."

JAPANESE MOTION GRAPHIC CREATORS 2012
2012—Book Cover
Client BNN, Inc. 4D2A
Design TYMOTE

Since the book is about a collection of Japanese motion graphic artists, TYMOTE composed a simple design by combining small visual elements of motion graphics.

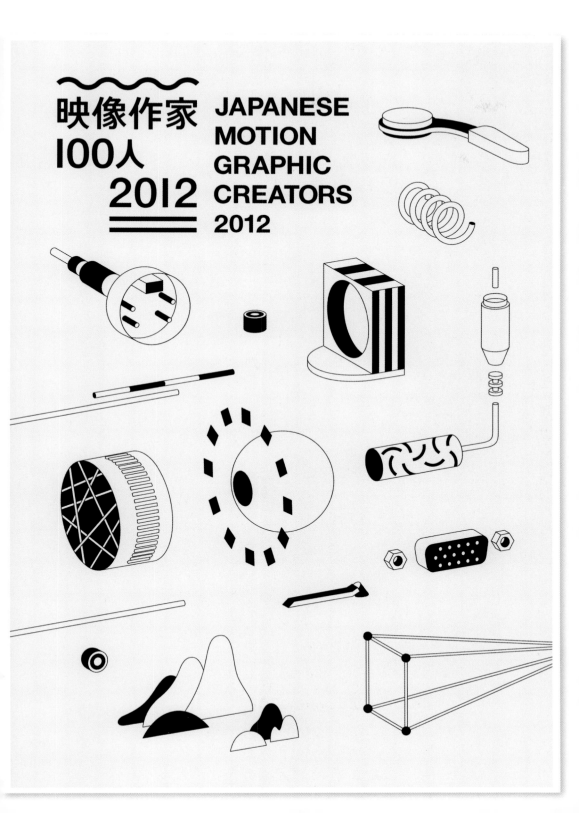

映像作家
100人
2012

JAPANESE
MOTION
GRAPHIC
CREATORS
2012

Re-Designing the East
Politisches Design in Asien und Europa
25. September 2010 – 9. Januar 2011
Württembergischer Kunstverein Stuttgart

Re-Designing the East
2010—Poster
Client Württembergischer Kunstverein Stuttgart
Design   L2M3 (Sascha Lobe, Dirk Wachowiak)

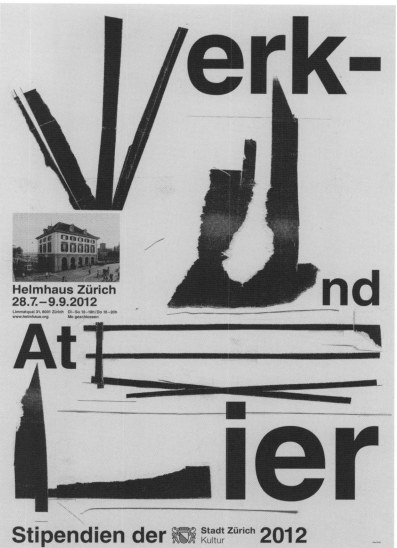

Helmhaus Zürich
28.7.–9.9.2012
Limmatquai 31, 8001 Zürich Di–So 10–18h/Do 10–20h
www.helmhaus.org Mo geschlossen

Stipendien der Stadt Zürich Kultur 2012

Typeface in Use
Helvetica LT

"Helvetica is the corporate font of the city of Zurich."

Werk- und Atelierstipendien der Stadt Zürich 2012
2012—Poster
Client Helmhaus Zurich
Design Atlas Studio

In a variety of typographical compositions, experimental letterforms and the official language of the city are combined to form the title of the show.

Werk un**d** **At**elier

Helmhaus Zürich
28.7.–9.9.2012
Limmatquai 31, 8001 Zürich   Di–So 10–18h/Do 10–20h
www.helmhaus.org   Mo geschlossen

Stipendien der Stadt Zürich Kultur **2012**

Sueh Li Tan's Favorite
Helvetica Letter is "A".

Typeface in Use
Helvetica Neue

"This assignment is about designer's personal favorite typeface. Helvetica was one of my favorite typefaces back then."

Helvetica
2007—Poster
Design Sueh Li Tan

A series of 6 posters were created to commemorate the 50th anniversary of Helvetica's introduction. Tan extracted selected little details of Helvetica that enthusiast her and elaborated them in the posters.

helvetica
vertical lines

These vertical lines are extracted from 'I'. The
vertical and horizontal lines of Helvetica are very
beautiful because they are the simplest form in
the whole family with absolutely precise
proportion. Helvetica has smooth, clean lines and
an unobtrusive geometry that almost suggests it
was designed not to stand out.

helvetica
horizontal lines

These horizontal lines are extracted from en dash.
The vertical and horizontal lines of Helvetica are
very beautiful because they are the simplest form
in the whole family with absolutely precise
proportion. Helvetica has smooth, clean lines and
an unobtrusive geometry that almost suggests it
was designed not to stand out.

helvetica
corners

These shapes are extracted from the joined part
of 'H'. The proportion of two strokes that joined
together looks just right. Helvetica has smooth,
clean lines and no unobtrusive geometry that
almost suggests it was designed not to stand out.

helvetica
counters

These circles are extracted from the counter of
'o'. The white shape of Helvetica is outstanding
and it holds the words together strongly. It has
quite a large counter space that make it very
legible. Helvetica has smooth, clean lines and an
unobtrusive geometry that almost suggests it
was designed not to stand out.

Typeface in Use
Helvetica,
Century,
DIN

"We wanted to use fonts that suit the warm visual image."

Cut, Paste, Collective
2012—Book
Client BNN, Inc.
Design TYMOTE, Ayame ONO

The pair has created a book that explains different collage techniques utilizing both digital and analog methodologies. Every artwork is composed in a manner to maintain the warm atmosphere created by analog representation.

Cover Magazine
Magazine
Client Malling Publications
Design Homework

Cover is Denmark's leading publication in
fashion, beauty and lifestyle, where avant-
garde meets mainstream, from lifestyle guru
Tyler Brülé's recommendation in the Finan-
cial Times to the front page of style.com.
Homework has undertaken the magazine's art
direction and graphic design to reflect their
vision and approach.

Helvetica Black
+
Caslon Grad
=
Helslon Black

Fontomixeur: Helslon Black
2011—Typography, Posters
Design Pierre Jeanneret

Fontoximeur is a project about mixing fonts. It analyzed two fonts of two distinct families to create a brand new typeface.

a + a = a
a a a a
e + e = e
e e e e
G + G = G
G G G G
N + N = N
N N N N

Caligraphie
Grotesk
parchemin
Alphabet
Humanistique
PLUME
contre-poinçon

Ee

Typeface in Use
Helvetica Black, Caslon Grad

"I needed two different kinds of font, one 'neutral' and one with a lot of contrast."

Champalimaud – Cancer Symposium
2009—Event Identity
Client Champalimaud Foundation
Design Studio Dumbar (Rejane Dal Bello)

The Champalimaud Foundation is a private organization that supports individual researchers and research teams working at the cutting edge of medical science.

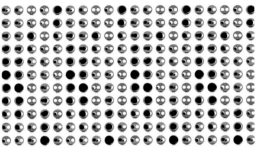

Typeface in Use
Helvetica Neue Bold

Amsterdam Sinfonietta Poster Series
2007-09—Poster
Client Amsterdam Sinfonietta
Design Studio Dumbar (Rejane Dal Bello)

Rejane Dal Bello's
Favorite Helvetica
Letter is "e".

Amsterdam Sinfonietta is an independent musical ensemble, mostly
consisting of young musicians. The two season poster collection
were developed during a period of two years.

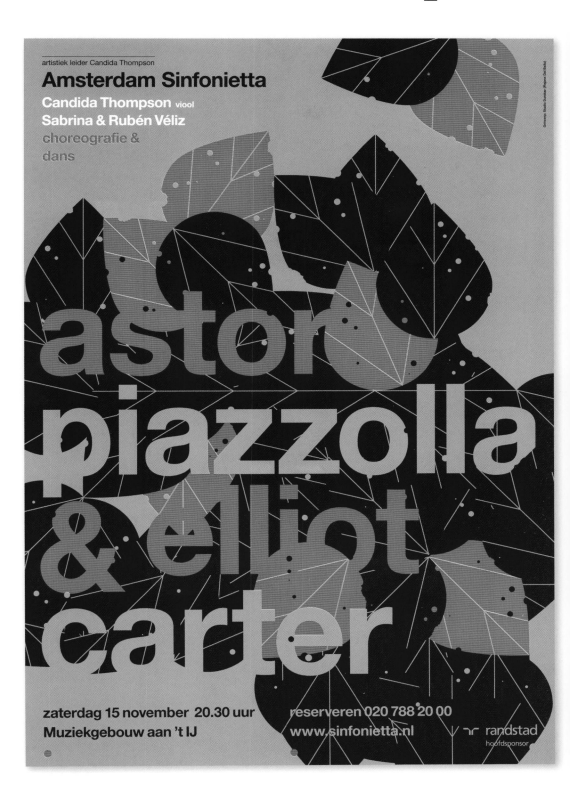

artistiek leider Candida Thompson

Amsterdam Sinfonietta

Candida Thompson viool
Sabrina & Rubén Véliz
choreografie &
dans

astor piazzolla & elliot carter

zaterdag 15 november 20.30 uur
Muziekgebouw aan 't IJ

reserveren 020 788 20 00
www.sinfonietta.nl

randstad
hoofdsponsor

Am sterdam sinfonietta

elegy for a rose

Candida Thompson,
leiding & viool

vrijdag 7 oktober 20.15 uur
Muziekgebouw aan 't IJ

James Gilchrist, tenor
Jasper de Waal, hoorn

reserveren 020 788 20 00
www.sinfonietta.nl

Amsterdam Sinfonietta

Brahms zwanenzang

Candida Thompson,
leiding & viool

vr 5 oktober 20.15 uur
Muziekgebouw aan 't IJ

Patricia Kopatchinskaja, viool
Viktor Kopatchinsky, cimbalom

reserveren 020 788 20 00
www.sinfonietta.nl

Ravel
Tsjaikovski
Beethoven

Natalia Gutman

Celloconcert
Saint-Saëns

**Candida Thompson,
leiding & viool**

vr 24 februari 20.15 uur
Muziekgebouw aan 't IJ

reserveren 020 788 20 00
www.sinfonietta.nl

Amsterdam Sinfonietta

lento religioso

Candida Thompson, leiding & viool

vr 12 mei 20.15 uur
Muziekgebouw aan 't IJ

Severin von Eckardstein, piano

reserveren 020 788 20 00
www.sinfonietta.nl

Typeface in Use
Helvetica

WAT DOET HIJ WAT DOET ZIJ WAT DOET ZIJ

JIJ DOET OOK HIJ DOET OOK ZIJ DOEN OOK

"Helvetica is the best typeface to communicate this statement for the characteristic strengths it has, like the heavi-, hard- and bold- ness."

2

Be original
2007—Poster
Design SuperBruut (Thijs Janssen)

SuperBruut's Favori
Helvetica Number is

Mini poster series about the power of copycats and movement of the bigger group. The red poster is readable in different ways, and says the same thing every time. The poster says: What I do, He does too, What he does, does she too, what see does, do they too. The black poster contains an equivoke that says: copycats are herd animals.

COPYCATS ARE HERD ANIMALS

"The corporate line of the theatre company is made only in Helvetica so we kept the idea to use only this font to create the poster for this play."

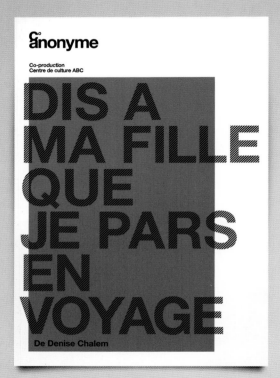

Co
anonyme

Co-production
Centre de culture ABC

DIS A MA FILLE QUE JE PARS EN VOYAGE

De Denise Chalem

Femmes en prison :
L'histoire poignante de deux
détenues que tout sépare et qui
vont se prendre d'amitié.

MISE EN SCÈNE
Matthieu Béguelin
JEU
Rachel Esseiva,
Maya Robert-Nicoud,
Nathalie Sandoz
LUMIÈRES
Gilles Perrenoud
DÉCORS
Yvan Schlatter
SONS
Stéphane Mercier

Avec le soutien de L'ABC,
du Canton de Neuchâtel,
de la Ville de la Chaux-de-
Fonds, de la Ville de
Neuchâtel, de la Loterie
Romande, de la Banque
Cantonale Neuchâteloise,
du Bistrot du Concert.

Co-production Centre
de culture ABC

LA CHAUX-DE-FONDS / Rdv au Temple-Allemand
22-23-24-29-30 novembre et 1er décembre 07   20h00
25 novembre et 02 décembre 07   17h00

EXPOSITION AUTOUR DE LA PIÈCE
Vernissage au Temple-Allemand à La Chaux-de-Fonds le 22
novembre 07h00 à 18h00. L'exposition est ouverte les jeudis
et vendredis dès 18h00 ainsi que les samedis et dimanches
dès 14h00.

RÉSERVATIONS ET INFOS
La Chaux-de-Fonds   +41 (0) 32 967 90 43

NEUCHÂTEL / Caves du Palais
06-07-08-13-14-15 décembre 07   20h00
09-16 décembre 07   17h00

EXPOSITION AUTOUR DE LA PIÈCE
Vernissage aux Caves du Palais à Neuchâtel le 06 décembre
07h00 à 18h00. L'exposition est ouverte les jeudis et vendredis dès 18h00 ainsi que les samedis et dimanches dès
14h00.

RÉSERVATIONS ET INFOS
Neuchâtel   +41 (0) 79 213 43 57

EXPOSANTS
Alessandra Respini
Collectif Doux-Jésus
Massimiliano Baldassarri
Studio 41
Guillaume Perret

Collectif Anonyme
2007-08 — Poster
Client Collectif Anonyme
Design Chris Gautschi

Typeface in Use
Helvetica Neue 55 Roman,
Helvetica Neue 75 Bold

The play is about being in prison so it would be logical to use a typography that is neutral and cold. Gautschi kept the idea to use the typeface in only two weights and have some-thing straight, clear and precise with a strong impact.

Cie anonyme

MISE EN SCÈNE
Matthieu Béguelin
JEU
Rachel Esseiva, Maya Robert-Nicoud, Nathalie Sandoz
LUMIÈRES
Gilles Perrenoud
DÉCORS
Yvan Schlatter
SONS
Stéphane Mercier

LA CHAUX-DE-FONDS / Rdv au Temple-Allemand
22-23-24-29-30 novembre et 1er décembre 07   20h00
25 novembre et 02 décembre 07   17h00

EXPOSITION AUTOUR DE LA PIÈCE
Vernissage au Temple-Allemand à La Chaux-de-Fonds le 22 novembre 07h00 à 18h00. L'exposition est ouverte les jeudis et vendredis dès 18h00 ainsi que les samedis et dimanches dès 14h00.

RÉSERVATIONS ET INFOS
La Chaux-de-Fonds   +41 (0) 32 967 90 43

NEUCHÂTEL / Caves du Palais
06-07-08-13-14-15 décembre 07   20h00
09-16 décembre 07   17h00

EXPOSITION AUTOUR DE LA PIÈCE
Vernissage aux Caves du Palais à Neuchâtel le 06 décembre 07h00 à 18h00. L'exposition est ouverte les jeudis et vendredis dès 18h00 ainsi que les samedis et dimanches dès 14h00.

RÉSERVATIONS ET INFOS
Neuchâtel   +41 (0) 79 213 43 57

Avec le soutien de L'ABC, du Canton de Neuchâtel, de la Ville de la Chaux-de-Fonds, de la Loterie Romande, de la Banque Cantonale Neuchâteloise, du Bistrot du Concert.

Co-production
Centre de culture ABC

DIS A MA FILLE QUE JE PARS EN VOYAGE

**Femmes en prison:
L'histoire poignante
de deux détenues que tout
sépare et qui vont se prendre
d'amitié.**

de Denise Chalem

Graphisme www.chilliepunch.ch

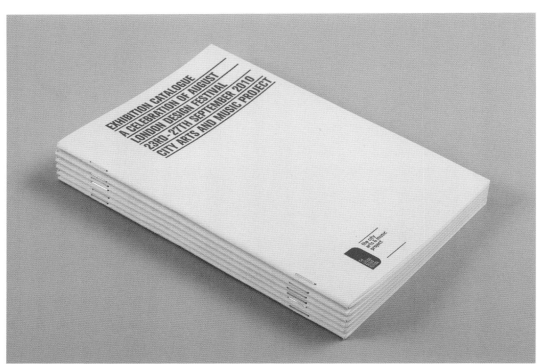

Typeface in Use
Helvetica Neue

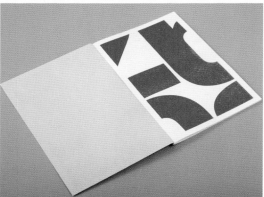

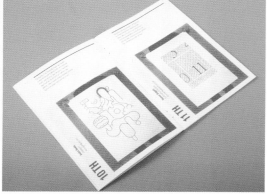

Celebration of August
2011—Visual Identity Design Mortar&Pestle Studio

Identity for a poster exhibition as part of the London Design Festival. The event showcased 30 designers and illustrators. Each exhibitor was asked to create an A1 poster about a specific day in August, which then assembled to become a calendar.

With a huge array of styles and techniques by the different exhibitors, Mortar&Pestle Studio chose Helvetica for its neutrality, which would take the work to become a talking point at the exhibition.

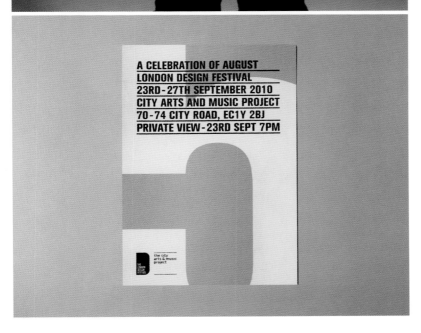

Labour Market Intelligence
2010—Brochure
Client Skillfast-UK
Design The Consult

Aimed at careers advisers with no previous knowledge of the fashion and textile sector, the Labour Market Intelligence document was a report full of facts and figures relating to the fashion and textile industry. The commission's brief was to design a visually powerful, accessible and engaging publication to help career professionals understand this complex industry so they could advise their clients appropriately. With no budget for photography or illustration, data was presented in a number of graphical ways, emphasizing key facts, setting the pace of the document and adding variety to the publication. The use of large scale format, and micro diecut detailing, ensured the report gained the desired response.

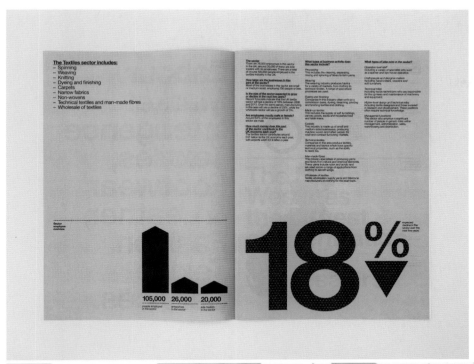

"It has the clarity and impact needed to effectively communicate the statistics throughout the publication."

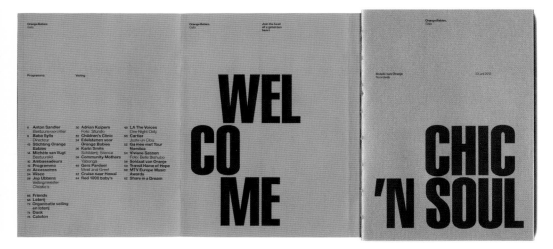

"Orange Babies
already had its iden-
tity established in
Helvetica, we wanted
to stay truthful to
this throughout
further executions,
as Helvetica embod-
ies the seriousness
of all projects very
well. For the Orange
Babies Gala 2012 we
were looking for a
typeface with a "New
York Street" feel –
big, bold and monu-
mental. It should hold
strong enough for
various type-only full
page designs."

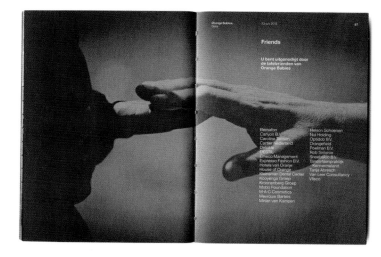

Typeface in Use
Helvetica Neue 55 Roman,
Helvetica Neue 75 Bold,
Helvetica Extra Compressed

Orange
2011-12—Visual Identity
Client Orange Babies
Design Carsten Klein

Orange Babies is a foundation helping pregnant women with HIV and their babies in Africa. To raise money via various events they set up and support a great number of projects in Africa. The biggest event is their annual charity ball targeting to seek funds from celebrities and wealthy members of society. This event conceived its own identity, themed Chic'n Soul in 2012. Orange Babies makes a bold effort in linking charity work with those of wealth. This requires the design to steer away from the organic and low-cost feel generally associated with charities in general to something just that is just glamorous and chic.

Pro Helvetia 1939 to 2009 – Between Culture And Politics
2010 — Book
Client Pro Helvetia
Design Raffinerie AG für Gestaltung

The 334-page bulk reader was published in three languages (German/French/Italian), covering 70 years of history of the Swiss arts council, Pro Helvetia. The authors succeeded to have a critical and all-embracing view on a piece of Swiss cultural funding. The multilingual ribbon bookmarks symbolize the typical Swiss trilingual culture. The font Raffinerie AG für Gestaltung used for the text is Helvetica 55 Roman, which stands for successful international Swiss design. The front pages of the different parts of the book are held in Syntax Letter, also developed by a Swiss artist. Another special detail of the book is, that the title layers are based on hanging initials that crowd themselves out. Besides the texts a selection of posters reduced to black and white shows projects which have been supported by the foundation throughout the time.

Typeface in Use
Helvetica 55 Roman,
Syntax Letter

WHO RUNS THE SPACE NOW?

⟨ A NINO BAUMGARTNER ⟩

⟨ B GWENAEL BELANGER ⟩

⟨ C YOAN CAPOTE ⟩

⟨ D ZILVINAS KEMPINAS ⟩

⟨ E KARYN OLIVIER ⟩

ECOH GALERIA / MEXICO
NEUE GALERIE / SWITZERLAND

Typeface in Use
Helvetica

"Representing the Swiss part of the collaboration."

Atlas Studio's
Favorite Helvetica
Letter is "e".

WhoRunsTheSpaceNow
2012—Editorial
Client Neue Galerie (CH), ECOH Galeria (MEX)
Design Atlas Studio

Publication accompanying the exhibition
WhoRunsTheSpaceNow, co-organized by
the Neue Galerie and ECOH Galleria in
Mexico City.

Kreissparkasse Ludwigsburg
2007—Signage System
Client Kreissparkasse Ludwigsburg
Design L2M3 (Sascha Lobe, Frank Geiger)
Architecture KBK Architekten Belz | Lutz
Photography L2M3 (Florian Hammerich)

The conceptual design of a functional and branded guidance system demonstrated pre-distorted labelings of the floors and staircases so that they can be perceived correctly from one point and change into free play of form otherwise. The savings banks, acting independently of one another, are each searching for their own local reference. For Ludwigsburg, on the one hand, the conceptual approach "Baroque", with its architecturally mediated delusions of the eye, is definitive for the main design theme; on the other, it is the architectural characteristic of a 140m long access corridor that ties together the various new buildings.

Typeface in Use
Helvetica Neue, Helvetica Light,
Helvetica Medium

It's A Small World
Exhibition Design
Client Danish Design Centre
Design Homework

It's A Small World explores new perspectives in Danish design, craft and architecture. With focus on Sustainability, Human Scale, New Craftsmanship and Non-Standardized Praxis, the exhibition challenges the traditional role of the designer. Six interdisciplinary scenarios seek a new relevancy for design - in the world. The exhibition is organized as a collaboration between Danish Design Centre, Danish Crafts and Danish Architecture Centre and is generated from an initiative in the Ministry of Economic and Business Affairs and the Ministry of Culture in Copenhagen, Shanghai, Brazil, Chile.

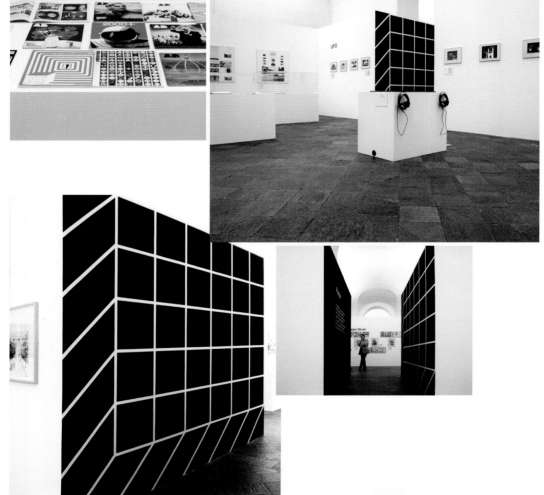

Contesto

La rivoluzione sessuale, l'invenzione della minigonna, le occupazioni delle università per una migliore didattica, gli scioperi e le lotte operaie, l'ondata rivoluzionaria proveniente dal campus californiano di Berkeley, le proteste contro la guerra in Vietnam e la musica, rappresentano il contesto degli anni Sessanta in cui prende forma l'architettura radicale.

9999
Archizoom
Pietro Derossi
Ugo La Pietra
Gianni Pettena
Superstudio
Gruppo Strum
UFO
Zziggurat

Radical
City

Radical City
2012—Visual Identity, Exhibition
Client Ordine Architetti Torino
(OAT) & (FOAT)
Design Artiva Design
(Daniele De Batté, Davide Sossi)

Radical City is the title of the exhibition on the Italian Radical architecture at the "Archivio di Stato" in Turin. The graphic identity reveals a modular structure; a white grid on black evocative of the Superstudio project, "Monumento continuo".

Discoteca

La discoteca è il luogo dove i giovani possono esprimere la loro creatività al pari dei coetanei inglesi e americani. È lo spazio del coinvolgimento sensoriale: il Piper.

Typeface in Use
Helvetica Bold

"Simple and strong!"

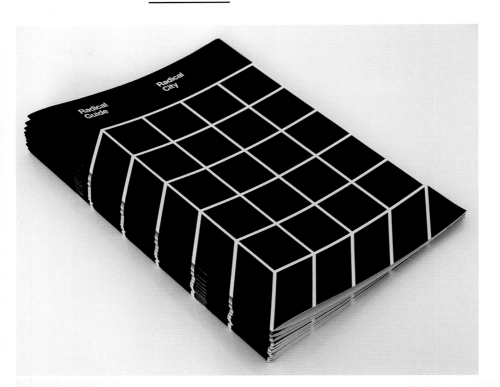

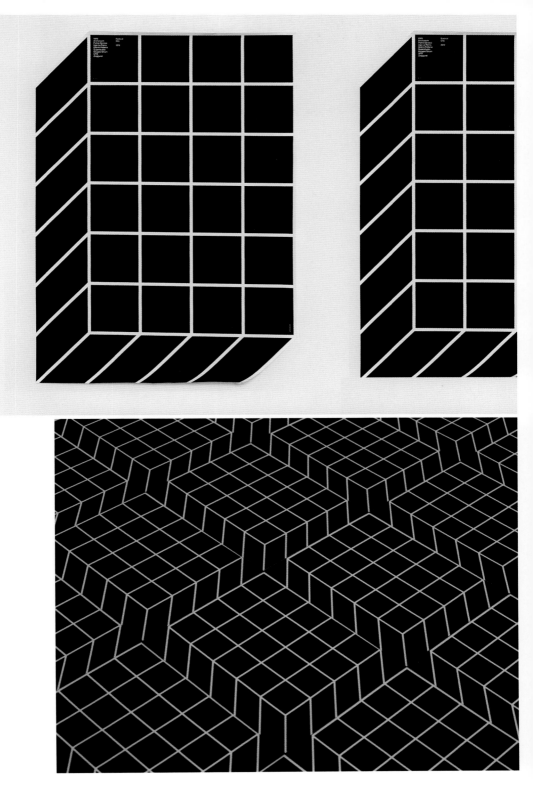

Typeface in Use
Helvetica Neue Bold

"Because of its origin
& usability."

SOYU – Creative Zodiac
2012—Poster
Client SOYU
Design Chris Henley

The brief was to create a piece inspired by
one animal from the Chinese Zodiac, with
influences from Asian-inspired art, blending
the East and the West.

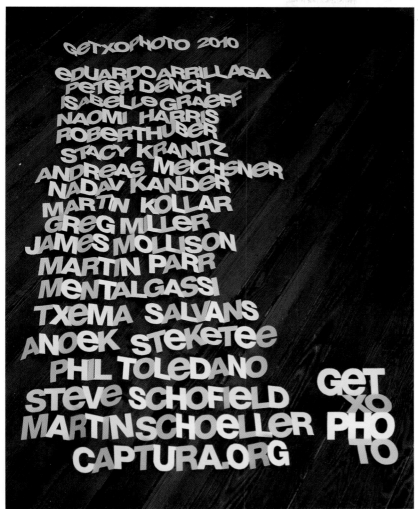

Paper Chain Type
2011—Visual Identity
Client Getxophoto
Design Is Creative Studio (Richars Meza)

GETXOPHOTO is a festival dedicated to photography that takes place in Getxo (Basque Country) and supports the exploration of formats, stands and unconventional exhibition spaces to show the different images.
The festival Getxophoto's 2010 theme was "In praise of leisure" — the moment dedicated to self-realization. The typography played a big role on the design, expressing the theme concept and representing the leisure in a bold and simple way so it could be applied to the sign system and communication pieces.

Is Creative Studio custom-made the type elements from cut paper and folded them like the paper doll chain like the children's craft. The sign system was based on the typography "Paper Chain Type" derived from Helvetica.

Helvetica 50
2008—3D Type
Design Make Studio

Typeface in Use
Helvetica

As a celebration of Helvetica's 50th anniversary, Make Studio produced an art piece using its traditional form but modernized with volume to promote their services with subtle references to is Swiss origin.

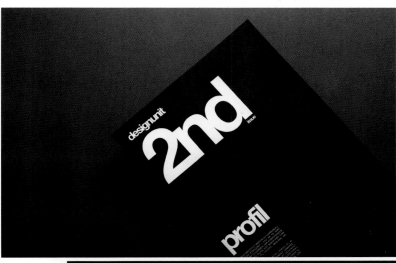

Self promotion
2006—Catalog
Design DesignUnit
(Jesper Johansen)

Catalogs for self pro-
motion made in A2
format.

Typeface in Use
Helvetica

"It's clean, efficient and minimalistic."

Tea
2007—Visual Identity
Client Tea Limited
Design Mind Design

Identity and overall design concept for a chain of tea shops, simply called 'Tea'. The first shop is located next to Saint Paul's Cathedral in London, a popular tourist destination. The idea of the logo is that the inner part of the letter 'a' forms the tea leaf and changes color according to the type of tea. The color scheme is used to categorize similar type of teas and make the rather complex world of tea more accessible. The identity has been applied to packaging, menus and interior graphics. Occasionally the clean typographic design is contrasted by references to old-fashioned English tea culture such as tea cozies and doilies.

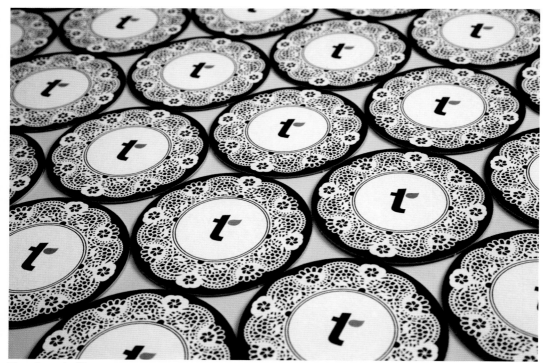

Typeface in Use
Helvetica Neue 75 Bold,
Helvetica Neue 45 Light

"The counter of the lowercase 'a' looks like a leaf, a tea leaf in this case. We also wanted to create a clean and functional identity."

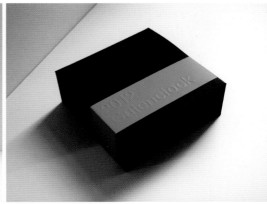

Typeface in Use
Helvetica

Antalis Calenclock 2012
2012—Calendar
Client Antalis(HK)Limited
Design BLOW (Ken Lo)

We were asked to design a calendar which is lifestyle and functional. We found that there is an interesting relationship between 12 months in the calendar and 12 hours on the clock. Inspired by this relationship, we designed a calendar with an embedded clock. Each month is also given a lighthearted wording related to individual months.

Hell Yes!
2011—Poster
Client 3001
Design Denise Franke

Hell yes! was a poster campaign composed for 3001, a club for electronic music in Düsseldorf, Germany.

Tuttobene all-in-one newspaper
2007—Exhibition Identity, Publication
Client Tuttobene
Design Lesley Moore
Photography Alberto Ferrero

For the 2007 Milan Furniture Fair, Lesley Moore designed Tuttobene's presentation with just one element — the 'all-in-one' newspaper. A handle-like cut-out made it possible to hang the newspaper on the exhibition walls. A range of functions were created by re-ordering the pages of the newspaper in various ways, including signage, catalog, flyer, plan, slogan, wallpaper and posters for individual designers.

Typeface in Use
Helvetica Neue Bold,
Times New Roman

"Tuttobene is a design organization we liked using the two archetypical fonts Helvetica and Times"

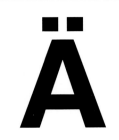

Everything's Favorite
Helvetica Letter is "Ä".

Everything Christmas 2010 Promo
2010—Packaging
Design Everything

Everything wanted to wish their clients a
merry (but responsible) Christmas in 2010,
giving rise to a gift that arrived in a box titled
"Everything in moderation". The contents
were a set of beers labelled "Everything in
moderation... Lessons 1". The reverse labels
featured a visual narrative beginning with
Santa's Christmas night, enjoying a little
tipple and a mince pie left on a family's table
and ending in a bit of a mess.

*"We've always used
Helvetica as Every-
thing's typeface."*

Typeface in Use
Helvetica Neue

sistema contra incendios

salida

teléfono público

libro di colorimiento

extinguidores

baño privado

Baño de Mujeres

doutor

dentista

Baño de Hombres

doutora

niño

Paz Holandesa (Free Children's Hospital)
2010–12—Visual Identity
Client Paz Holandesa
Design Rejane Dal Bello

Paz Holandesa is a non-profit Children's hospital in Arequipa, Peru. With Yomar
Augusto Rejane Dal Bello sponsored the identity design for this hospital. It was
a great working process with the creator of the hospital (Marjan van Mourik) who
is devoted to this amazing project and is inspirational for the development of the
design. Initiated in 2005 the ongoing visual identity solution includes logo, sta-
tionery, folders, cards and signage, wall paintings, games, editorial.

Typeface in Use
Helvetica Neue Bold

"When I look at the Helvetica, I think it is the one of the most neutral typeface. Because of its variety of usage, we might forget about the original form of the font. For this project, I want to make an instruction book people can confess about their sexual life. Therefore I chose Helvetica which looks indifferent on their privacy."

How Far Did You Go: 1 to 24
2009—Book, Information display design
Design Studio DD (Min Jae Huh)
Photography Young Hoon Kim

Participants were asked a series of personal, somewhat embarrassing questions, and could only give (honest or dishonest) answer "yes" or "no" indicated by color stickers on a poster. An example of mixed facts and fictions created by anonymous crowd. Illustration was based on Cosmopolitan and collage by Min Jae Huh.

Typeface in Use
Neue Haas-Grotesk

"Neue Haas-Grotesk is a revival of Helvetica, 135
drawn by Christian Schwartz. We wanted
to use a popular typeface, which can be as
neutral as possible."

SNACK Ombragé A 100 m.

Tout le monde connaît Roger Excoffon
2011 — Poster
Client Tony Simões Relvas, Samuel Rambaud
Design Clément Le Tulle-Neyret, Thomas Leblond

Poster for the participation in exhibition Tout
le monde connaît Roger Excoffon, Musée de
l'imprimerie de Lyon in 2012.

Mut zur Wut 2012
2012—Poster
Client Mut zur Wut (Götz Gramlich)
Design Felix Pfäffli

A poster for the international poster contest "Mut zur Wut". Entrants are completely free in the choice of topic for their poster design. The brief of the exhibition "Mut zur Wut (Courage to rage)" required critical, social or personal reference in the form of a graphical or illustrative motif.

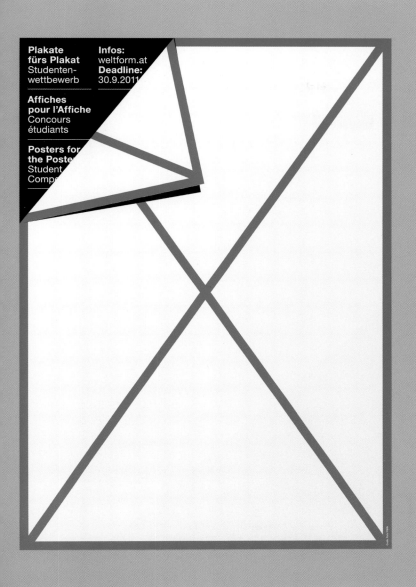

**Plakate
fürs Plakat**
Studenten-
wettbewerb

Infos:
weltform.at
Deadline:
30.9.2011

**Affiches
pour l'Affiche**
Concours
étudiants

**Posters for
the Poster**
Student
Comp...

Posters for the Poster
2011—Poster
Client Weltformat
Festival
Design Felix Pfäffli

Posters for the Poster is a poster for a poster contest. There is a huge archive of posters alike but this work has conceived the title "Posters for Posters" as two mirrors confronting each other that creates an endless tunnel. I found that a lot designers made the wrong decision in that situation. Stressing communication, this poster is all about the free space to design.

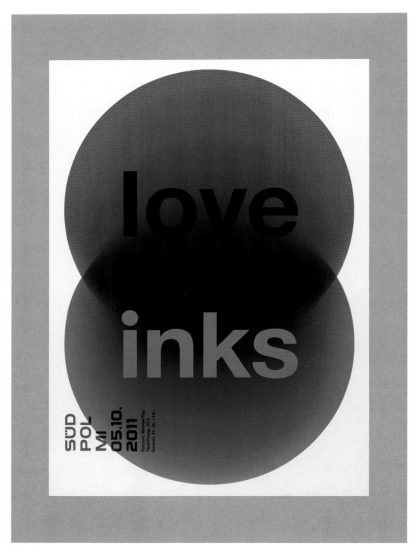

Südpol Posters
2011—Poster
Client Südpol
Design Felix Pfäffli

Suedpol is a multipurpose cultural center in Kriens, Switzerland, that houses a theater, a symphony orchestra, a brass band, a music school, a restaurant, a flea market, and rents its rooms for performances of music, dance, theater, literature, digital arts and so on. The concept for that poster series was originally designed by Erich Brechbühl. After working with his concept over a year, I transformed it this summer into a very free construction. The only guidelines are now the previously defined font family, the font size for the medium text and the risograph technique. Where everything else — position, color, shape — may vary, Felix Pfäffli calls that corporate diversity, a corporate design that sets you no useless boundaries to really illustrate the content. Simplified, a corporate that is as free as possible.

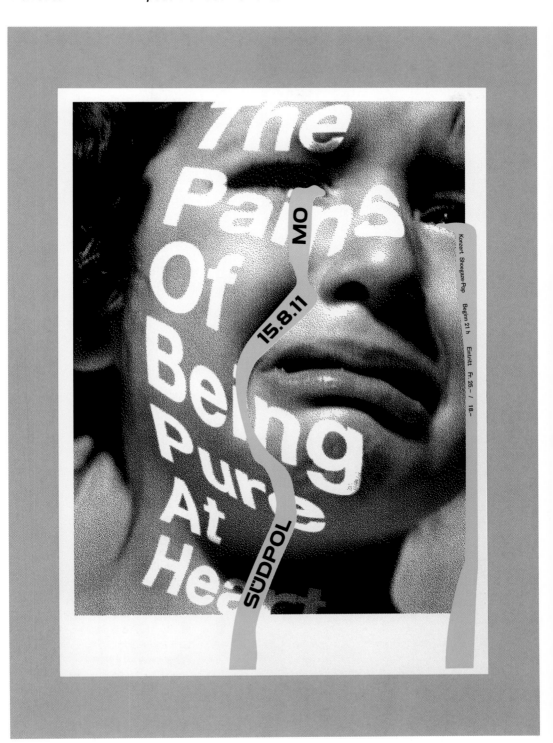

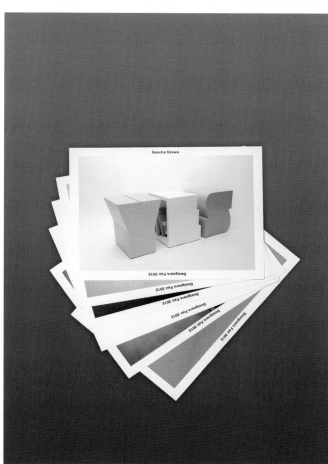

Designers Fair 2012
2012—Visual Identity
Client heimatdesign
Design David Latz,
Dennis Wedding

DESIGNERS FAIR is an annual interior design fair Cologne, Germany. The solution contains a website, an exhibition catalog in form of a newspaper, an information booklet and postcards for every exhibition.

Typeface in Use
Helvetica Neue Light,
Helvetica Neue Bold

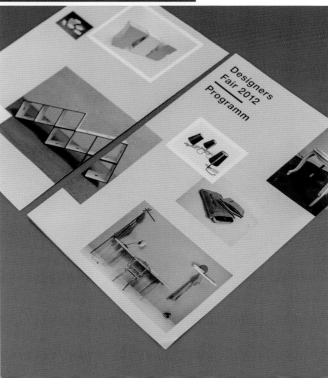

2

Blockprojects
2011—Visual Identity
Client Blockprojects gallery
Design Studio Worldwide

Blockprojects gallery has provided a creative hub for
Australian artists since the 1990s. Rather than moving
away totally from their three dimensional wordmark, Studio Worldwide simplified it into a bold icon suggestive of
their space. This direction was then explored across all
collateral with a clean gridded approach allowing the artists' work to be the hero.

*"This typeface was
used to allow the
'Block' icon and art-
ists imagery to drive
the direction of the
brand communica-
tions."*

Blockprojects
—

Robert Jacks
Cut & Tied
—

22 Aug / 15 Sep 2012
—

+613 9429 0660
79 Stephenson St
Richmond
Australia 3121
—

Opening times
Wed / Fri   11 / 5 pm
Sat   11 / 4 pm
Sun   12 / 4 pm
—

info @
blockprojects.com
—

A	H	Open	V
Bend	Insert	P	Weld
Cut	J	Q	X
D	K	Roll	Y
E	L	Stretch	Z
Fold	M	Tie	
G	N	U	

from Listings (1970)

A recipe for... Robert Jacks: Cut & Tied

Not long after arriving in New York, in the latter half of 1969, Robert Jacks began working on what might be described as a suite of experimental poems. While in some ways this turn to a focus on words might seem at odds with a career founded in painting and sculpture, these textual experiments actually sit quite comfortably within the broad range of activities that constituted his practice at the time.

Collected together in 1970 under the title "Listings", each piece plays with small clusters of conceptually connected words inserted into a neatly typed vertical alphabet - in much the same way as his studio practice repeated patterns and processes across a range of materials. By following a simple recipe, it becomes possible to evoke quite a lot with just a few words, such as this piece which builds quite a narrative in just three carefully selected words: "A/B/C/D/Eggs/F/G/H/I/J/K/L/M/N/Omelette/P/Q/R/Salad/T/U/V/Weld/X/Y/Z". Other pieces explore fields of meaning in more static ways, or by seeming to offer possibilities for action. Perhaps one of the most striking is "A/Bend/Cut/D/E/Fold/G/H/Insert/J/K/L/M/N/Open/P/Q/Roll/Stretch/Tie/U/V/Weld/X/Y/Z", a sequence which seems to echo the range of strategies Jacks was exploring in the production of his sculptural work at the time.

These days it is difficult to avoid the link between the second of these pieces and Richard Serra's well known text based work "Verb List Compilation: Actions to Relate to Oneself" (1967-1968), which begins "to roll/ to crease/ to fold/ to store/ to bend..." with the list finally finishing over a hundred items later with "to continue". Having made the link, it is important to note that, despite the superficial similarities between the two "lists", it is highly unlikely that Jacks was even aware of Serra's piece when he wrote his.

Certainly, the ideas both pieces embody, were "in the air", and the broad circulation of Serra's hand written text did not occur until an extract of it was published in the second issue of the art journal Avalanche in 1971 (which is where Jacks recalls seeing it for the first time). While Jacks' list is these days presented as an important "working drawing" for key works that followed it, part of the cannon of conceptual art (in fact, an "original" hand written version is held in the collection of the MOMA in New York), in Jacks' case, the little alphabet poem remains virtually unknown.

There is, however, a relationship between text and artwork in Jacks' practice that has its roots in a project he began almost immediately after his first highly successful solo exhibition of paintings at Melbourne's Gallery A in 1966. This project - "An Unfinished Work" - is primarily sculptural, but has produced outcomes that range from artists' books and drawings to work in three dimensions. It also makes extensive use of text to map out the form of each sculptural object. It is a project that seems to fit within the broad paradigm of conceptual art outlined by Sol LeWitt in his seminal "Paragraphs on Conceptual Art", first published in Art Forum in the Summer of 1967: "When an artist uses a conceptual form of art, it means all of the planning and decisions are made before hand and the execution is a perfunctory affair. The idea becomes a machine that makes art".

But while the experiments embodied in "An Unfinished Work" do broadly sit within the context of minimal and conceptual art, Jacks' practice tends to sit a little to one side of the pure threads of either of these movements. It probably always has. As Ian Burn noted in his 1970 essay "Conceptual Art as Art": while "much of Robert Jacks' recent work has moved beyond painting into conceptualised presentations of numerical systems and serial techniques... such art is closer to a kind of process art than it is to a stricter definition of conceptual art".

In retrospect, these sorts of technical definitional quibbles seem less significant than the early response to the work, and the context in which it was developed. In 1971 Jacks' was selected by Sol LeWitt and Robert Rauschenburg to present his work as part of a suite of solo exhibitions at the New York Cultural Centre, an opportunity that allowed him to show a number of cut pieces in paper and felt as well as the artists' books which included working "drawings" and specifications for the works. From the point of view of the artist, the various different ways of presenting the work all had an equivalence, with the description being seen as equal to the manufactured work. But while some conceptualists, like LeWitt, normally leave the execution the art object to others, this is rarely the case with Jacks.

As an on-going project, "An Unfinished Work" remains true to its title. Across the early 1970s Jacks continued to develop the various threads within the project with a number of focussed exhibitions in New York and Canada, and over the last three decades has returned to it on numerous occasions. Of course, there is quite a difference between the visual elegance of a work hanging on the wall, and confronting a set of instructions and specifications typed out on a quarto page. Over the years Jacks has produced work that explores the sculptural possibilities embodied within "An Unfinished Work", producing pieces in a wide range of materials, and at quite different scales. He has also continued to develop the artists' book that operates as the foundation of this project, publishing a variety of extracts and editions since in 1970.

A number of the works in this exhibition are directly linked to the pieces in one of his first artists' publications, Twelve Drawings, which is focussed on the work originally produced under the title "Modular II 1968 - 1970. In a similar way, the pieces in this exhibition use a range of materials, each of which offers a different response to the underlying conceptual framework. While it may not be obvious at first glance, the formal structure played out within these angular cut pieces and grid based works is also found within the tied forms. These latter works are a kind of deconstruction or framework for the works the textual element of the project seeks to describe. Hanging as they do, these tied works might remind us of the flat paper patterns used by tailors and fashion designers to assist in cutting out the fabric for suits or dresses, which is then stitched together to form the three dimensional garment.

But, as we all know in these days of competitive cooking shows, having a recipe and the right ingredients isn't always enough to make a top chef's signature dish. And as truly creative cooks have found, the more you experiment with the basic ingredients the better the eventual results. Like a master chef, Robert Jacks has been working with both the ideas and execution of these works over many decades, and he knows the recipe by heart. During his career, he's also been willing to admit other flavours, to spend periods of time engrossed in the nuances of adjacent cuisines. But these, I think, are some of his "classic dishes".

Peter Anderson

Resurexit:
The Eradicate

Bernhard
Sachs
30 May —
23 Jun
2012

Reception
Sat 02 Jun
2 — 4 pm

It Never
Came

Conor
O'Brien
25 Jul —
15 Aug
2012

Exhibition
Opening
Drinks

Reception
Sat 28 Jul
2 — 5 pm

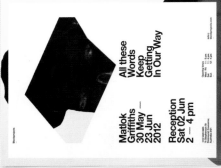

All these
Words
Keep
Getting
In Our Way

Matlok
Griffiths
30 May —
23 Jun
2012

Reception
Sat 02 Jun
2 — 4 pm

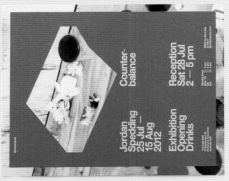

Counter-
balance

Jordan
Spedding
25 Jul —
15 Aug
2012

Exhibition
Opening
Drinks

Reception
Sat 28 Jul
2 — 5 pm

Black
Magic

26 May

Reception

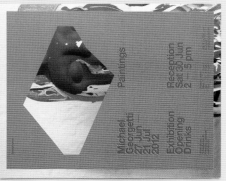

Paintings

Michael
Georgetti
27 Jun —
21 Jul
2012

Exhibition
Opening
Drinks

Reception
Sat 30 Jun
2 — 5 pm

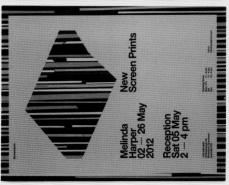

New
Screen Prints

Melinda
Harper
02 — 26 May
2012

Reception
Sat 05 May
2 — 4 pm

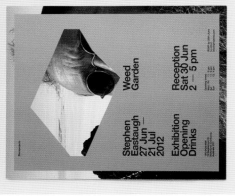

Weed
Garden

Stephen
Eastaugh
27 Jun —
21 Jul
2012

Exhibition
Opening
Drinks

Reception
Sat 30 Jun
2 — 5 pm

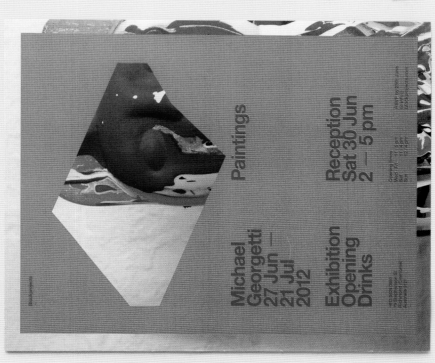

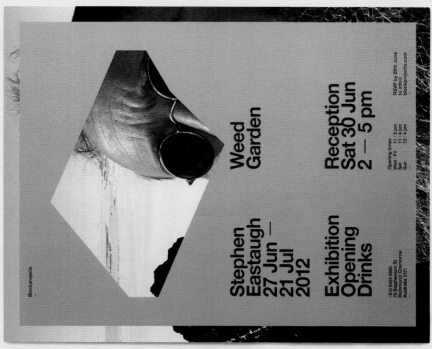

a

Studio Worldwide's
Favorite Helvetica
Letter is "a".

"This typeface was used to be as quiet as possible, while providing the bold geometric W for the self promotional poster."

Studio Worldwide
2010—Visual Identity, Poster
Design Studio Worldwide

The first poster in the series was an announcement about the inception of Studio Worldwide in Australia and a call for clients. The text side described the studio's approach and the graphic side was a visual joke based on the geometry of a snowflake, a comment from the European designers on the unusually hot Australian Christmas launch.

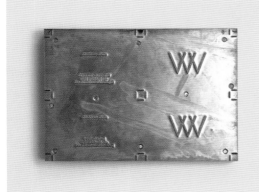

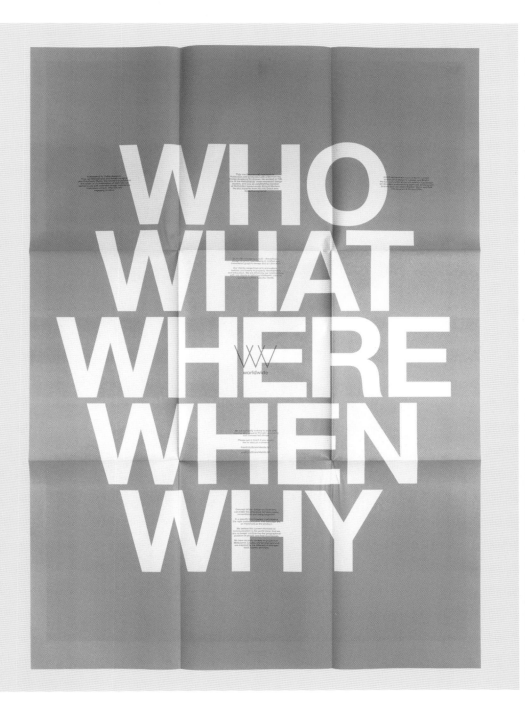

louise blanche
2009-12—Visual Identity
Client louise blanche
Design Burri-Preis

louise blanche is a playful Swiss
textile label. Main elements are
apples who return in different
ways and dots in the typeface.

Typeface in Use
Customized
Helvetica Neue

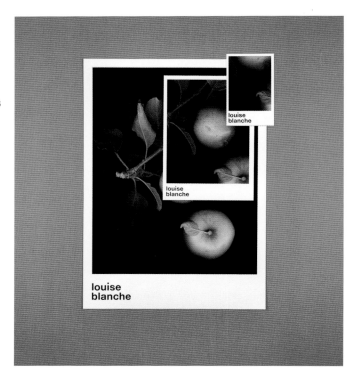

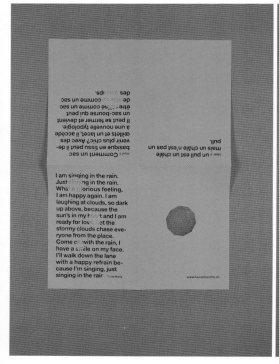

"*louise blanche is a playful Swiss textile label. Helvetica, as the name already says, is very Swiss, the round dots give it a playful touch.*"

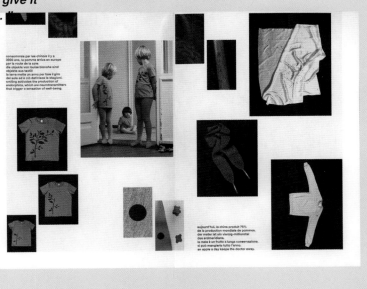

Andrés Requena
andresrequena.es

Andres Requena is from Barcelona. He believes in the shape's synthesis as a way of explicit and direct communication, avoiding needless visual elements. He always tries to add objectivity to his work facing the lack of real information and dissembled advertising that we are submitted every day.
— pp. 56-57

Artiva Design
artiva.it

Artiva Design is a multidisciplinary studio doing graphic design, branding and visual communication. Based in Genoa (Italy), it was founded in 2003 by two designers, Daniele De Batté and Davide Sossi. Basically the projects are focused on the presence or absence of graphic elements in geometry and on the use of a rigorous grid system that shows their natural bent towards minimalism.
— pp. 116-119

Atlas Studio
atlasstudio.ch

ATLAS is a Zurich based graphic design studio founded by Martin Andereggen, Claudio Gasser and Jonas Wandeler. They work for clients in both commercial and cultural fields. Their service includes printed and digital matter such as publications, identities, posters or websites. Besides that they pursue self-initiated projects and collaborations on an regular basis.
— pp. 83-85, 112-113, 116-119

BLOW
blow.hk

BLOW is a Hong Kong based design studio founded by Ken Lo in 2010. They are specialized in branding, identities, packaging, environmental graphics, publications and web design.
— p. 125

Bunch
bunchdesign.com

Bunch is a creative design studio offering a diverse range of work, including, identity, literature, editorial, digital and motion. Established in 2002 with an international reach, from London to Zagreb.
— pp. 44-45, 59, 74-75

Burri-Preis
burri-preis.ch

Burri-Preis are two graphic designers based in Zurich, Switzerland. They are collaborating since 2008 on printed matter, such as books, posters, logos, flyers and sometimes they even do websites.
— pp. 154-155

C100 Purple Haze
c100purplehaze.com

C100 Purple Haze is a Munich based multidisciplinary design consultancy founded by Christian Hundertmark and Clemens Baldermann. The studio's diverse output includes projects for miscellaneous public and private clients on a variety of national and international projects including expertise in conception, art direction, typography, design and illustration.
— pp. 76-79

Chris Gautschi
chrisgautschi.ch

Chris Gautschi is a Swiss graphic designer. He lives and works in the district of East London, UK. He studied graphic design at l'Ecole d'Arts appliqués, La Chaux-de-Fon, Switzerland. Passionate about typography, he uses it to nurture and grow his work. His passion is reflected by his clients through corporate identity, packaging, annual reports, brochures, etc.
— pp. 102-103

Chris Henley
24exp.co.uk

Chris Henley is a UK based freelance Graphic Designer, Illustrator and Art Director. With strong roots in the typographic, a mix of music, vintage style and humor help define his work which spans a wide range of creative disciplines.
— p. 120

Clément Le Tulle-Neyet
clement-ltn.com

Clément Le Tulle-Neyret is a graphic designer who studied graphic design at the Fine Art School in Lyon. He works most of the times typographically for various printed matter, such as books, magazines, visual identities, posters, record sleeves, etc.
— pp. 24-25, 135

**David Latz,
Dennis Wedding**
davidlatz.de
denniswedding.de

David Latz and Dennis Wedding studied communication design at the university of applied science in Dortmund, Germany.
— pp. 140-143

Denise Franke
dfact.de

Denise Franke is a freelance Art Director from Germany. She studied Communicationdesign at the Folkwang University of the Arts in Essen and works in various fields of design for agencies and individuals.
— pp. 126-127

DesignUnit
designunit.dk

DesignUnit is a creative fashion and branding agency, founded in 2006. The agency is experienced in defining and building brands and creating strategic campaigns and marketing solutions. These include product and packaging design, printing, ad campaigns, magazine design, book design, corporate identity, websites and shop image. The agency's brand-building expertise spans from fashion, and lifestyle to magazine development.
— p. 123

Everything
everythingdesign.co.nz

Everything are a graphic design company based in Auckland, New Zealand. They spend much of their time working on brand projects but like to design Everything.
— pp. 130-131

Felix Pfäffli
feixen.ch

Feixen is the graphic design work of Felix Pfäffli. Felix was born in 1986. In 2010 he graduated and started his own studio "Feixen". In the summer of 2011 he was appointed as teacher at the Lucerne School of Graphic Design to teach in the fields of typography, narrative design, and poster design.
— pp. 136-139

Hans Gremmen
hansgremmen.nl

Hans Gremmen (1976, NL) is a graphic designer based in Amsterdam. He works in the field of art, architecture and photography, and is one of the driving forces behind publishing house Fw:. A publisher focused on photography publications.
— p. 51

Henrik Nygren Design
henriknygrendesign.se

Henrik Nygren Design mainly deals with analysing the client's market potential, with strategy in accordance with this potential and the design and production of books, magazines, packaging, corporate identities, advertising campaigns and exhibitions.
— pp. 20-23, 26-33

Homework
homework.dk

Homework is a creative agency and design consultancy offering visual brand identity, packaging and advertising for the art, culture, fashion and luxury industry. Homework was founded in 2005 by Jack Dahl. He has worked as art director for mens fashion magazine HE, Intermission and Cover magazine. In addition, Jack Dahl has worked with Self Service magazine and the strategic and creative Paris agency Petronio Associates on a selection of fashion, beauty and luxury brands.
— pp. 62-67, 90-91, 115

Is Creative Studio
iscreativestudio.com

Is Creative Studio is an independent creative studio with global vison. With simplicity as our operating philosophy IS Creative Studio delivers services in brand identity and development, art direction, packaging, printed matter, interactive design, animation, art projects, exhibitions, fashion and product design. IS stands for secret ingredient, that unique "thing" in the soul of anyone driven to create with real passion, real originality. IS Creative Studio was established January 2010 by Richars Meza.
— p. 121

Keith Kitz
onemansstudio.com

One Man's Studio is the independent design practice of Keith Kitz, specializing in the creation of compelling visual solutions for a wide spectrum of clientele. Created on the belief that graphic design can change the world. Kitz sees his work as a personal calling to declutter the visual landscape, replacing distractions with thoughtfully executed expressions of beauty. Through his passion for design, he works to help educate others on the importance of their visual decisions, and guide them to the most impactful results.
— p. 43

Klein
carstenklein.com

Klein is an international graphic design consultancy, launched in London in 2002 by Carsten Klein. Now based in Amsterdam, it retains clients in the UK, The Netherlands, Germany and USA. It specialises in visual communication and brand identities with a strong focus on printed matters and typography, as well as websites, arts, and communications.
— pp. 52-55, 108-109

L2M3
L2M3.com

L2M3 Kommunikationsdesign is a graphic design agency with high standards of form and content. Founded by Sascha Lobe in 1999, the agency handles signage systems and graphic design for exhibitions in addition to traditional tasks such as developing corporate images and designing printed matter.
— pp. 82, 114

Lesely Moore
lesley-moore.nl

Lesley Moore is the brainchild of Karin van den Brandt (1975, Blerick, The Netherlands) and Alex Clay (1974, Lørenskog, Norway). Since studying at the Arnhem Academy of the Arts (now ArtEZ) their careers have been intertwined. Early cooperations include the design for the Academy's magazine 'De Kunsten'. In 2004 they went on to form Lesley Moore, the name referring to 'less is more'. This mentality can be detected on various levels in their work, but first and foremost in the minimalistic approach in the conceptual phase of the creative process.
— pp. 128-129

Loose Collective
loosecollective.net

Loose Collective is an independent creative studio based in Manchester, UK. They work with clients, both big and small, who are willing to think a little differently from the norm. They believe that great design and effective communication should always be built upon good ideas and not by succumbing to visual trends. They prefer not to follow the herd.
— pp. 46-47

Make Studio
makestudio.co.uk

Make Studio consists of a core of designers, directors, artists and creative thinkers with strong external links with printers and photographers to provide an integrated network.
— p. 122

Maureen Mooren
maureenmooren.nl

Maureen Mooren is a graphic designer based in Amsterdam, the Netherlands, where she runs her own studio. In her work Mooren, by definition raises the issue of representation. In recent years Mooren has worked as an guest tutor at Werkplaats Typografie in Arnhem, the Netherlands.
— pp. 68-73

Mind Design
minddesign.co.uk

Established in 1999, Mind Design is a design consultancy that specialises in the development of visual identities which includes print, web, and interior design. The studio is run by Holger Jacobs and Stewart Walker. Their approach combines hands-on craftmanship, conceptual thinking and intuition and develop visual ideas on the basis of research into production processes or the use of unusual materials. Depending on the demands of a project they take advantage of their network of creative professionals.
— p. 124

Mortar & Pestie Studio
mortarpestlestudio.com

Mortar&Pestle Studio is a multidisciplinary design consultancy based in London. The practice encompasses art direction, brand identity, marketing communications, design for print, web and environmental design.
— pp. 104-105

Oliver Daxenbichler
oliverdaxenbichler.com

Oliver Daxenbichler, founder of Oliver Daxenbichler associates, is a 35 year old Creative director and Graphic designer who lives and works currently in Frankfurt Main, Germany. Over the course of almost one decade he has been working on a variety of print and new media based projects including conceptualizing and producing ad campaigns and catalogues, logos and brand identities and magazine design.
— pp. 18-19

Pierre Jeanneret
pierrejeanneret.com

Pierre Jeanneret is a Swiss graphic designer, who has just finished his studies at the Écal (Bachelor of Arts HES-SO in Visual Communication) in Lausanne. He works on his own assignments as well as for various design agencies.
— p. 92

Raffinerie AG für Gestaltung
raffinerie.com

Raffinerie AG für Gestaltung was founded in March 2000. It is being directed by Reto Ehrbar and Nenad Kovacic (both founders and partners) and Christian Haas. They started small with three people, and grew constantly every year. At the moment they are 14 people, all graphic designers or illustrators. There is no such style as 'the Raffinerie style'. They try to come up with a new solution for every new client.
— pp. 110-111

Random Press
Sandra Doeller, Michael Satter & Marco Balesteros

Marco Balesteros started Random Press in partnership with Michael Satter and Sandra Doeller, a self-publishing project that coexists in Lisbon and Frankfurt, and aims to serve as a platform for irregular experiences in publishing, production and distribution of content.
— pp. 36-37

Rejane Dal Bello
rejanedalbello.com

Senior Graphic Designer and Illustrator Rejane Dal Bello has been based in the Netherlands since 2004. Originally from Rio de Janeiro, she began her career working for renowned branding & design companies in Brazil. After her BA in Graphic Design in Rio de Janeiro, Rejane went on to study under Milton Glaser at the School of Visual Arts in New York City. She completed a MA at Post St Joost Academy in The Netherlands in 2006. During her MA, Rejane joined Studio Dumbar. Rejane is based in the UK and currently a Senior Designer at Wolff Olins. Previously worked at Studio Dumbar for 7 years as well as a member of the faculty of Post St Joost Academy, where she teaches Graphic Design and Creative Process.
— pp. 132-133

Studio DD
studio-d-d.com

Min Jae Huh is running the design studio DD based in London, New York & Seoul. She was born in Seoul 1984, did a BA at the Rhode Island School of Design, and a MA at the Royal college of Art. Her work wants to initiate human communications. She wants to create an open platform which will help people to discuss and promote their opinions about current social and cultural issues. The platform is flexible so it can intervene in unexpected situations and locations.
— p. 134

Studio Dumbar
studiodumbar.com

Studio Dumbar is an international agency with a Dutch heritage. They describe their work as 'visual branding, online branding', meaning they create every visible expression of a brand or organization — offline and online. This involves strategy, communication, branding and process-management. They are located in Rotterdam, Shanghai and Seoul.
— pp. 93-99

Studio Worldwide
studioworldwide.net

Studio Worldwide is a multi-disciplinary design practice specialising in graphic design and art direction. Established by Dutch designer Thijs van Beijsterveldt and British designer Joel Priestland. Thijs van Beijsterveldt was born in Rotterdam and graduated with a BA from the Design Academy Eindhoven. Joel Priestland was born in North London and studied design in London and Bristol. Their clients range from arts and culture, fashion and luxury to property development and education.
— pp. 144-153

Sueh Li Tan
suehlitan.com

Sueh Li is a graphic and type designer from Penang, Malaysia. She holds a Masters in type design from the Type and Media Master program at the Royal Academy of Art in The Hague (KABK). She has collaborated with Sara de Bondt Studio, Martin Fröstner and Zak Group in a few custom type projects. In 2012, she co-founded Typokaki with Karmen Hui to explore type design and typography in relation to Malaysian cultures through workshops, events and research.
— pp. 86-87

SuperBruut
superbruut.nl

SuperBruut is... the most original, the idealist, the visionary, the number one and that guy who was, with his eight years, left behind at a reststop along the Belgian highway. These things aren't all entirely true, accept for the last one... Yes, he is that guy who was standing on a reststop crying. That guy who was picked up by the police. That guy who sat for four hours at the Belgian police station. That guy who was spoiled by the police with soda cans and chocolate bars. Nowadays that guy designs.
— pp. 100-101

Tankboys
tankboys.biz

Tankboys is a Venice-based independent design studio founded in 2005 by Lorenzo Mason and Marco Campardo. Tankboys' core activities consist of art direction, research, print, identity and editorial projects. Alongside with that, they give lectures, hold workshops and run a publishing house called Automatic Books.
— pp. 10-17, 60-61

The Consult
theconsult.com

The Consult is a team of brand and design experts. For the past decade they have been working for their clients and their brands. Understanding their market and strategic objectives is an integral part of their design process.
— pp. 106-107

Them Design
them.co.uk

Them are a London-based branding and design consultancy. They work with a diverse range of clients internationally. They are inspired by anything visual and love type, especially Helvetica, even using it in their own branding.
— pp. 38-41

Toby Ng
toby-ng.com

Toby Ng graduated in Graphic Design from Central St. Martins, London and he now lives in Hong Kong. Ng previously was associated with Sandy Choi Associates in Hong Kong and London design agencies such as Landor and Saatchi & Saatchi Design.
— p. 42

TYMOTE
tymote.jp

TYMOTE is a design bureau based in Tokyo. They center around graphic design and art works for motion graphics, computer graphics, music, interface designing and web designing.
— pp. 80-81, 88-89

Veronica Ditting
veronicaditting.com

Veronica Ditting (1979) is an art director working in Amsterdam and London. After graduating from the Gerrit Rietveld Academy, Amsterdam in 2005, she worked for a diverse range of clients from individuals to institutions, focusing mainly on printed matter. She is the art director of the magazines The Gentlewoman and Fantastic Man.
— pp. 34-35

Walter Santomauro
waltersantomauro.com

Walter Santomauro is a young graphic designer, born in Turin, whose curiosity and inclination towards the graphic area has been cultivated during his studies at Politecnico of Turin. He is attending the "Virtual and Graphic Design" course.
— p. 58

Workroom
workroom.kr

Located in Seoul, Korea, workroom is a graphic design studio and publishing house. In December 2006, four people—a photographer, an editor and two graphic designers—jointly opened the studio. Since then, workroom has primarily worked on community design and publishing as well as design services for clients. In addition, workroom helps run Gagarin, a second-hand bookstore opened in 2008 that specializes in art and design.
— pp. 48-50

First published and distributed by
viction:workshop ltd.

viction:ary™

Unit C, 7th Floor, Seabright Plaza,
9-23 Shell Street, North Point, Hong Kong
URL: www.victionary.com
Email: we@victionary.com
www.facebook.com/victionworkshop
www.twitter.com/victionary_
www.weibo.com/victionary

Designed & Edited by TwoPoints.Net
Preface by Indra Kupferschmidt
Images for preface by Linotype (www.linotype.com)

Typefaces in Use:
Helvetica Bold
Helvetica Bold Oblique

©2013 viction:workshop ltd.

ISBN 978-988-19439-4-1

Printed and bound in China

We would like to thank all the designers and companies
who made significant contribution to the compilation of
this book. Without them this project would not be able to
accomplish. We would also like to thank all the produc-
ers for their invaluable assistance throughout this entire
proposal. The successful completion also owes a great
deal to many professionals in the creative industry who
have given us precious insights and comments. We are
also very grateful to many other people whose names did
not appear on the credits but have made specific input and
continuous support the whole time.